Francis W. Doughty

The Cents of the United States

A Numismatic Study

Francis W. Dougthy

The Cents of the United States
A Numismatic Study

ISBN/EAN: 9783742860170

Manufactured in Europe, USA, Canada, Australia, Japa

Cover: Foto ©ninafisch / pixelio.de

Manufactured and distributed by brebook publishing software
(www.brebook.com)

Francis W. Doughty

The Cents of the United States

THE

CENTS OF THE UNITED STATES.

A NUMISMATIC STUDY.

EXTENSIVELY ILLUSTRATED FROM SELECTED SPECIMENS.

"Take care of the Cents and the Dollars will take care of themselves."

BY

FRANCIS WORCESTER DOUGHTY.

NEW YORK:
SCOTT STAMP AND COIN CO., L'D.
12 East 23rd Street.
1890.

TO

THE MEMORY OF ROBERT COULTON DAVIS,

TO WHOSE UNTIRING EXERTIONS IN THE PATHS OF

NUMISMATIC SCIENCE, IS LARGELY DUE THE PRES-

ENT ADVANCED KNOWLEDGE ENJOYED BY

AMERICAN COLLECTORS OF THE

INTRICACIES OF OUR NATIONAL

COINAGE.

INTRODUCTORY.

In preparing the present review of the favorite coin of our American collectors, the endeavor has been to produce a work which shall meet the wants of the advanced numismatist, whose desire it is to gather each die variety, and at the same time to offer to the amateur a guide to the cents of the United States which can be comprehended at a glance.

With the first end in view, exhaustive descriptions have been attempted of the cents issued from the United States mint between the years 1793 and 1814, inclusive, which embrace all the rarities of the series, with a carefully tabulated arrangement of those issued between 1816 and 1839, subsequent to which date interest diminishes. Between the years 1840 and 1857, the die varieties are too slight to warrant even the brief descriptions of the first table, and a second one less extended is substituted; while of the cents issued after 1857, no description has been attempted beyond a brief general notice. Interest in the issues of later years is too slight to call for extended investigation into the minute differences of the several dies employed.

To the amateur whose desires do not extend beyond the collection of types, the illustrations are offered and will be found to fully meet his wants. They have been prepared with more than usual pains, from carefully selected specimens, and although faulty in a few instances, afford by far the best series of pictures of the cents of the United States hitherto offered.

Although it is justly said that comparisons are odious, we feel that it is due to ourselves to direct the attention of collectors to the fact that the present work, modeled after the system adopted in the description of the cents of the United States published in The Coin

Collector's Journal during the years 1879, 1880, 1881, 1882 and 1883, is the nearest approach to a complete descriptive list of the interesting series treated in its pages, which has yet appeared. It began in the Journal in May, 1887, was continued until the suspension of that periodical in December, 1888, and is now offered to the public in its completed form.

Although perhaps unnecessary, we would call the attention of the collector to the method by which it is intended that the descriptions of the cents subsequent to the year 1794 should be used.

First carefully study the cent which it is desired to locate; if it offers any marked peculiarity, such as the blundered fraction, $\frac{1}{000}$, for instance, it can be readily placed. If this is not the case, take the measurements with a pair of dividers, jot them down, and beginning at the commencement of the descriptions of the year, continue until the measurements are found to correspond with some cent described.

By this method alone can the desired end be promptly attained, and collectors have our assurance that after a little practice all apparent difficulties will vanish. Do not attempt to locate cents by simply reading the descriptions; hopeless confusion can alone result.

It is a matter of regret that the incorrect figures of the mint reports, purporting to represent the number of cents issued each year, should have been repeated in this work. It is true that these figures have appeared in previous descriptions of the cents of the United States, and at the time our list began in The Coin Collector's Journal, it was deemed best to insert them. They are not to be relied upon, and should have been excluded.

Interest in our pleasing science is steadily increasing; yet in spite of the restricted limits of the numismatic history of our country, the field has been but imperfectly explored. It is, however, a favorable indication of more systematic methods of collecting on the part of American numismatists, that for many years there has been a constant and ever-increasing demand for a comprehensive treatise on the Cents of the United States.

THE

CENTS OF THE UNITED STATES.

A NUMISMATIC STUDY.

At the close of the Revolutionary war, one of the earliest subjects engaging the attention of the Continental Congress was the establishment of a standard coinage, which should supersede the Colonial paper issues and the clipped and worn Spanish silver coins then circulating throughout the country; and, more particularly, the innumerable counterfeit English halfpennies which had long clogged the tills of retail merchants, growing to be a positive nuisance, for these being of short weight and redeemable nowhere, formed a decided tax upon trade. The accomplishment of this desirable object was attended with much difficulty, and a full decade was destined to elapse subsequent to the establishment of peace between England and her colonies ere the foundations of a National coinage were finally laid. Meanwhile the newly formed States and private individuals were busy. Massachusetts, Connecticut, Vermont, New Jersey and Virginia all issued copper coins of about the size and weight of the English halfpenny; in addition to which speculative persons struck tokens and so-called patterns, some under state sanction, others not, and these, during the ten years between 1783 and 1793, were circulated with more or less freedom throughout the United States.

The year 1793 put a period to this irregular state of affairs, and became notable as marking the beginning of our National coinage by the issue of a copper piece under the name of *Cent*; a cognomen for a copper standard which during the following century was destined to extend itself, under numerous varying forms, among many of the nations of the civilized world.

The origin of the cent is to be found fully described in *Dunlap's American Daily Advertiser*, Philadelphia, February 9, 1791; being embodied in the report of Alexander Hamilton, Secretary of the Treasury of the United States. Such matter as relates directly to the coinage of the cent found in that report we offer herewith:

"With regard to the number of different pieces which shall compose the coins of the United States, two things are to be consulted, convenience of circulation and cheapness of the coinage. The first ought to be sacrificed to the last; but, as far as they can be reconciled to each other, it is desirable to do it. Numerous small, if not too minute, subdivisions assist circulation, but the multiplication of the smaller kinds increases the expense. * * The following [coins] it is conceived will be sufficient in the commencement. One gold piece equal in weight or value to two units or dollars. One gold piece equal to a tenth part of the former, which shall be a unit or dollar. One silver piece, which shall also be a unit or dollar. One copper piece, which shall be of the value of a hundredth part of a dollar. One other copper piece, which shall be of half the value of the former. The largest copper piece will nearly answer to the half penny sterling, the smallest, of course, to the farthing. Pieces of very small value are a great accommodation and the means of beneficial economy to the poor, by enabling them to purchase in small quantities, and at a more reasonable rate the necessaries of which they stand in need. If they are only cents, the lowest price for any portion of a vendible commodity, however inconsiderable in quantity, will be a cent; if they are half cents, it will be a half cent; and, in a great number of cases, exactly the same things will be sold for a half cent, which, if there were none, would cost a cent. * * The dollar is recommended by its correspondency with the present coin of that name, the Spanish American piece of *eight reales*, for which it is designed to be a substitute which will facilitate its ready adoption as such in the minds of citizens. The *disme*, or tenth, the *cent*, or hundredth, the *mille*, or thousandth, are proper because they express the proportions they are intended to designate. * * The word *cent*, being already in use in various transactions and instruments, will, without much difficulty, be understood as the hundredth, and the half cent, of course, as the two hundredth part. * * It is conceived that the weight of the cent may be *eleven pennyweight*, which will about correspond with the value of the copper and the expense of coinage. This will be to conform to the rule of intrinsic value, as far as regard to the convenient size of the coins will permit; and the deduction of the expense of coinage in that case will be the more proper as the copper coins which have been current hitherto have passed till lately for much more than their intrinsic value. Taking the weight as has been suggested, the size of the cent may be very nearly that of the piece herewith transmitted, which weighs 10 *dwt.* 11 *grs.* 10 *m.* Two-thirds the diameter of the cent will suffice for the diameter of the half cent."

Such, in condensed form, was the result of the ten years' deliberation of Congress concerning the establishment of our National coinage. During the century to follow, the issue of cents was destined to continue; and, as these coins form the basis of the greater proportion of the cabinets of our American collectors, it seems highly desirable that some properly tabulated list of dates and varying dies should be issued for their guidance. By no publication or individual has this ever been attempted with anything even approaching completeness save the *Coin Collector's Journal* alone. This list began in 1879 and was continued until 1883, describing all then known types and varieties of the United States cents, between the years 1793 and 1857. At the request of a large number of our subscribers, we have decided to traverse this field a second time, employing all valuable material contained in our previous list, with the addition of such new data as may subsequently have been brought to light. The arrangement will be by consecutive numbering; reverse varieties to be designated by letters. Preceding the description of the cents of each year will be explanatory remarks upon types, while such notes and comments will follow as may be deemed appropriate. The degree of rarity will be indicated by the letter R with superior figures attached, ranging from R^1 to R^8 That is, R^1 designates a variety which is entirely common, R^8 rarity in the highest degree. A particularly valuable feature will be the illustrations which have been especially engraved for the work in hand from the best specimens in existence. In their preparation neither time nor expense has been spared, and, in the majority of instances, they will be found to correspond accurately with the descriptions; all omissions and variations, of which unfortunately there are a few, will be carefully noted in the text.

The value of a list of the cents of the United States thus illustrated cannot be over-estimated. It meets a want long experienced by collectors, and, when completed, will form a guide to this typical coin of our country without whose aid no cabinet can be properly arranged.

1793.

There are three types of the cent of 1793. To these have become attached the names *Chain*, *Wreath* and *Liberty Cap*. We will now describe the varying dies under their respective heads.

No. 1.

REV. A.

CHAIN CENTS.

No. 1.—Obv. Head of Liberty to right. Above the head, LIBERTY In ex., 1793 The head presents a face not unhandsome, but with forehead highly receding. The hair is cut short, and hangs dishevelled as though facing a strong gale. The lowest lock points to the figure 1 in date. The letters in LIBERTY are regular and evenly spaced. The date is widely spaced, the figure 9 being slightly below the upper line of the 3.

Rev.—*Rev. A.*—UNITED STATES OF AMERI. Within a chain of fifteen links: ONE | CENT | $\frac{1}{100}$ A dot between the E and N just below the upper line of those letters—not represented in the illustration.

Edge.—A slender vine with leaves and bars arranged in alternate sections. R^6.

No. 2.—Obv. Same as No. 1.

Rev.—*Rev. B.* (See No. 3)

Edge.—A vine and bars. R^4.

No. 3.

REV. B.

No. 4.

No. 3.—Obv. Head of Liberty to right. Above the head, LIBERTY In ex., 1793 The head presents a countenance of more character than last; the hair is finer and hangs well to the left of the figure 1 in date; the extreme point of the neck is nearly above the figure 3. The word LIBERTY is composed of letters of uneven size widely spaced. The R in LIBERTY is larger than its fellows and stands above the upper line. The date is bold. but unevenly spaced, the 9 and 3 being closer than the 1 and 7.

Rev.—*Rev. B.*—UNITED STATES OF AMERICA Within a chain of fifteen links, ONE | CENT | $\frac{1}{100}$

Edge.—A vine and bars. R^3.

No. 4.—Obv. Head of Liberty to right. Above the head, LIBERTY. In ex., 1793. The face is less pleasing than in No. 3; the hair is abundant and long, extending nearer to the rim than represented in the illustration. The letters in the word LIBERTY are barely spaced at all, the L being slightly below the upper line; there is a period after Y. The date is arranged much the same as No. 3, the figure 9 and 3 are even closer; there is a period after the 3.

Rev.—*Rev. B.*

Edge.—A vine and bars. R^4.

These cents are all struck upon thick planchets and vary in size from 25 to 27½ millimeters, or from 16 to 16½ on the American scale.

WREATH CENTS.

No. 5. REV. C.

No. 5.—Obv. Head of Liberty to right. Above the head, LIBERTY Below, a sprig of four laurel blossoms. In ex., 1793 The face is of the same general character as in preceding numbers. The hair being less clearly cut presents the appearance of thick locks, the lowest of which almost touches the rim of the coin. The word LIBERTY is unspaced; the 9 in the date is larger than the other figures.

Rev.—*Rev. C.*—UNITED STATES OF AMERICA Within a wreath of laurel tied at the base with a ribbon, ONE | CENT The wreath is close and differs materially from all others of the type. About on a line with the loop of the ribbon, which is depressed to left of centre, are, to right, *two* laurel blossoms; to left, *one*. Sprays of berries are plentiful, one pointing downward toward the N in ONE is omitted in the illustration. The word ONE and CENT are close together and placed out of the centre, being nearer to the top of the wreath. In ex., $\frac{1}{100}$

Edge.—A vine and bars. R^8.

This and the following number are the rarest of the cents of 1793. No perfect specimens are known; that from which our engraving was prepared being the best. It is probable that there are *four* laurel blossoms in the wreath on the reverse, two on either side of the loop. As it is possible to distinguish but one on the left, however, we have preferred to so state it, subject to correction should a perfect specimen ever appear. The sprig beneath the head on the obverse is usually called a clover leaf, and from this these cents have acquired the name of the "Clover Leaf" variety. The writer of our former list termed it a "strawberry plant with three leaves and a berry." We must, however, dissent from both the usually accepted designation and that of the former editor of the JOURNAL. Comparison with the laurel blossoms in the wreath upon the reverse of this cent, shows them to be identical with the sprig in question; hence we shall term this piece and its companion, No. 6, the Laurel Blossom Cents.

No. 6.—Obv. Similar to No. 5. The top of the forehead points between the E and R in LIBERTY.

Rev.—*Rev. D.*—Similar to No. 5. The ONE | CENT stands nearer the centre of the wreath. The top of the laurel blossom on the left of the loop being nearly on a line with the centre of the letter C in CENT.

Edge.—A vine and bars. R^8.

No. 7.

REV. E.

No. 8

No. 7.—Obv. Head of Liberty to right. Above the head, LIBERTY Below, a sprig of laurel leaves. In ex., 1793 The letters in LIBERTY are large and widely spaced, the same being true of the figures in the date. The laurel sprig is composed of three broad leaves, widely and evenly separated, the stem pointing toward the figure 7.

Rev.—*Rev. E.*—UNITED STATES OF AMERICA Within a wreath of laurel leaves, blossoms and berries, tied at the base with a ribbon, forming a double loop, ONE | CENT Below the wreath, $\frac{1}{100}$ The upper blossom on the outside, to the left, is a little above the line of the C in CENT. The double loop marks a peculiarity in this variety which distinguishes it from all other reverses of the *Wreath* type. There is a minute dot between the E and N in CENT.

Edge.—A vine and bars. R^3.

No. 8.—Obv. Head of Liberty to right. Above, LIBERTY Below, a sprig of laurel leaves. In ex., 1793 The letters in LIBERTY are small and but slightly spaced. The figures of the date are small, regular and widely spaced. The top of forehead points between T and Y The sprig of laurel is of similar appearance to No. 7, but the stem is directed between the 7 and 9.

Rev.—*Rev. E.*

Edge.—A vine and bars. R^4.

No. 9. REV. F.

No. 9.—Obv. Head of Liberty to right. Above the head, LIBERTY Below, a sprig of laurel leaves. In ex., 1793 The letters in LIBERTY are small and widely spaced. The top of the forehead points between the R and T. The stem of the laurel sprig extends downward between the 7 and 9; the first leaf is nearly at a right angle with its fellows, extending toward the left. The date is more evenly spaced than appears in the illustration.

Rev.—*Rev. F.*—UNITED STATES OF AMERICA Within a wreath of laurel leaves, blossoms and berries, tied below with a ribbon, ONE | CENT Below the wreath, $\frac{1}{100}$ The loop of the ribbon is thick and slightly depressed in the centre. The laurel blossoms, of which there are four, are nearly on a line with CENT, the inner, left hand blossom being lower than the others and almost touches the C. A leaf touches the O in ONE, of which word the letters are unevenly spaced, the O and N being closer than the N and E. The legend is nearer the wreath than in the numbers which follow. A minute dot over N.

Edge.—A vine and bars. R^5.

REV. G.

No. 10.

REV. H.

No. 10.—Obv. Head of Liberty to right. Above the head, LIBERTY Below, a sprig of laurel leaves. In ex., 1793 The face is handsome, the eye appears to look upward; the top of the forehead is immediately beneath the R; the lower locks of the hair touch the beaded circle around the rim of the coin. The letters in LIBERTY are small and rather more evenly spaced than is represented in our illustration. The laurel sprig is composed of three small, thin leaves with a curved stem, almost touching the top of the 9 in its curvature, the point then rising above the 3. A small, lateral stem is projected from it to the left, toward the 7. The left hand leaf touches the hair. The figures of the date are regular and evenly spaced.

Rev.—*Rev. G.*—UNITED STATES OF AMERICA Within a wreath of laurel leaves, blossoms and berries, tied at the base with a ribbon, ONE | CENT Below the wreath, $\frac{1}{100}$ The four blossoms in the wreath are on a line with CENT. The bow is large and depressed to the right of centre. The fraction is small and the figures exceedingly close. There is a minute dot over N in CENT, another between the N and E in ONE.

Edge.—A vine and bars. R[3].

No. 11.—Obv. Same as No. 10.

Rev.—*Rev. H.*—UNITED STATES OF AMERICA Within a wreath of laurel leaves, blossoms and berries, tied at the base with a ribbon, ONE | CENT Below the wreath, $\frac{1}{100}$ The left branch of the wreath has twelve leaves and three blossoms; the right, fourteen leaves and two blossoms. Figures in fraction are well spaced and the dividing line curved. The bow is large and depressed in centre. There is a dot between the E and N of cent. A crack in the die extends diagonally from the wreath between the E and N of CENT. The upper spray of berries on the left points directly to the lower bend of the letter S of STATES. Edge: same as No. 10. R^3.

S-11 No. 12. Rev. I.

No. 12.—Obv. Head of Liberty to right. Above the head, LIBERTY Below, a sprig of laurel leaves. In ex., 1793 The letters in LIBERTY are small and evenly spaced. There is to be found on perfect specimens a small mark over the I which has been described as a dash. The laurel sprig is composed of three leaves inclined strongly to the right, the stem almost touching the figure 9. The date is small and widely spaced, the figure 1 being very close to the hair.

Rev.—*Rev. I.*—UNITED STATES OF AMERICA. Within a wreath of laurel leaves, blossoms and berries, tied at the base with a ribbon, ONE | CENT Below the wreath, $\frac{1}{100}$ The loop is lightly struck in centre, and generally appears divided as represented in our illustration. The dividing line of fraction is curved—not straight as depicted—and is usually so faint as to be almost unnoticeable. The letters of the legend are rude and the entire workmanship of inferior quality. There is a small dot directly above and touching the N of CENT.

Edge.—ONE HUNDRED FOR A DOLLAR This inscription reads on some specimens from right to left, on others from left to right. R^4.

LIBERTY CAP.

No. 13.—Obv. Head of Liberty to right. Behind the head, on the left, is a short staff supporting a Liberty Cap. Above the head, LIBERTY In ex., 1793 The head is of better artistic design than on preceding numbers, being larger and with a face possessing more character. The hair is gathered back from the forehead and confined by a narrow ribbon, from below which it hangs loose, but in more

No. 13. Rev. J. No. 15.

graceful curves than is the case with the "Flowing Hair" varieties. The word LIBERTY is unevenly spaced, as represented in the illustration; the letter L is very close to the dotted border.

Rev.—*Rev. J.*—UNITED STATES OF AMERICA Within a wreath of laurel leaves, blossoms and berries, tied below with a ribbon, ONE | CENT Below the wreath, $\frac{1}{100}$ On the right branch of the wreath are five berries; opposite the O in OF is a group of three leaves; the tip of a leaf *almost* touches the base of T of CENT [not so represented in the illustration]; the end of the ribbon touches the dividing line of the fraction.

Edge.—ONE HUNDRED FOR A DOLLAR R^5.

No. 14.—Obv. Same as No. 13.

Rev.—*Rev. K.*—This reverse differs from *Rev.* J. (the illustration) in the following particulars: Has only one leaf opposite the O in OF; tip of leaf is to the right, above the base of T of CENT; the end of the ribbon on the right extends below the dividing line of the fraction; a leaf opposite the right foot of the letter M of AMERICA.

Edge.—ONE HUNDRED FOR A DOLLAR R^6.

No. 15.—Obv. Head of Liberty to right. Behind the head, on the left, is a short staff supporting a liberty cap. Above the head, LIBERTY In ex., 1793 In general design this obverse is the same as No. 13. Its differing particulars are as follows: A line extending entirely across the planchet passing through the letter E of LIBERTY and immediately behind the figure 3 in the date, caused by a crack in the die. The E of LIBERTY is below the line of the other letters, and the entire word, the letters of which are otherwise even, further removed from the dotted border; the pole supporting the liberty cap is not deeply cut, causing it to strike up weakly, in some specimens being almost invisible.

Rev.—*Rev. J.*

Edge.—ONE HUNDRED FOR A DOLLAR. R^6.

No. 16.—Obv. Head of Liberty to right. Behind the head, on the left, is a short staff supporting a Liberty Cap. Above the head, LIBERTY In ex., 1793 In general design this obverse is the same as No. 15. Its differing particulars are as follows: A slight crack in the die shows as a line extending from the dotted border to the forehead, touching the right side of the letter Y of the word LIBERTY which is well removed from the border, as in No. 15; the letter E of LIBERTY is on a line with its fellows.

Rev.—*Rev. J.*

Edge.—ONE HUNDRED FOR A DOLLAR R^7.

No. 17.—Obv. Same as No. 16.

Rev.—*Rev. K.*

Edge.—ONE HUNDRED FOR A DOLLAR R^7.

The five varieties of the Liberty Cap cent present, as will be seen, differing points so slight as to be scarce distinguishable. It is believed that all were from one *hub die*, the various differing points being the work of the graver. The reasons for this belief, seem conclusive. They are as follows: 1. The facial expression, arrangement of hair, cap and pole are identical on all the specimens known. 2. The position of the head in reference to the date and word LIBERTY is invariably the same. 3. The circle forming the border is in every instance composed of ninety-five pellets or dots. The points of difference, are almost microscopic and can only be determined by actual measurement with a pair of dividers, for the reason that a specimen which has been circulated to any considerable extent will appear to the unaided eye decidedly different from a fine, sharp specimen produced from the same die.

From the source quoted at the commencement of our work, *Dunlap's American Daily Advertiser*, we extract the following additional particulars in relation to the cents of 1793:

"An act approved April 2d, 1792, Section 10, reads: 'That upon said coins respectively there shall be an impression emblematic of Liberty, with an inscription of the word Liberty and the year of the coinage; and upon the reverse of each of the copper coins shall be an inscription which shall express the denomination of the piece, namely, *cent*, or *half cent*, as the case may require.'

"An act approved May 8th, 1792, reads: 'The Director of the Mint with the approval of the President of the United States, be authorized to contract for the purchase of a quantity of copper, not exceeding one hundred and fifty tons, and that the said Director, as soon as the needful preparation shall be made, cause the copper by him purchased to be coined at the mint into *cents* and *half cents*, which shall be paid into the Treasury of the United States, thence to issue into circulation.

"That after the expiration of six months from the time when there shall have been paid into the Treasury by the said Director in *cents* and *half cents* a sum not less than fifty thousand dollars, which time shall forthwith be announced by the treasurer in at least two newspapers, published at the seat of the Government of the United States, for the time being, *all copper coins*, or pieces whatsoever, except the said *cents* and *half cents* that shall pass current as money, or shall be paid, or offered, or received in payment, contrary to the prohibition aforesaid, *shall be forfeited*, and every person by whom any of them shall have been so paid, offered, or received in payment, shall also forfeit the sum of ten dollars, which forfeit and penalty shall and may be recovered with costs of suit, for the benefit of any person who shall give information of the occurence.'"

In the same publication, issue of September 1, 1792, is to be found the following advertisement:

THE HIGHEST PRICE
Will be Given for
OLD COPPER
At the Mint,
North Seventh Street, No. 29. *September* 1, *eot.*

The first purchase of copper in accordance with this advertisement was on September 11, 1792—six pounds. Immediately after that date the price of the metal advanced and the standard weight of the cent was reduced to eight and two-third *dwt.* and the half cent in proportion, on January 26, 1796—the legal weight of the cent was still further reduced by proclamation of President Washington, to seven *dwt.* It retained this weight until the final abandonment of the large cent in 1857.

The first record of the number of cents coined is dated March 1, 1793, when the chief coiner delivered to the Treasurer 11,178 cents.

1794.

The number of die varieties of the cents of 1794 exceeds that of any other year. In general the obverses resemble the Liberty Cap type of 1793; the differing points being the size and appearance of the head; the spacing of the word LIBERTY; size and shape of the letters and their relative positions toward the head, cap, or border; size, form and position of the figures of the date and the lines caused by broken dies.

In the description of both obverse and reverse die impressions, we shall as a matter of space economy omit repetition of the legends, etc. Let it be understood that all cents of the year 1794 bear upon the obverse the head of Liberty with the cap upon the short pole behind, on the left; the word LIBERTY above and the date 1794 below; while on the reverse is the legend: UNITED STATES OF AMERICA, with ONE | CENT within a wreath of laurel leaves, blossoms and berries, tied at the base with a ribbon, between the pendant ends of which is the fraction $\frac{1}{100}$ Upon the edge the incuse legend ONE HUNDRED FOR A DOLLAR invariably occurs. Upon some specimens, the reading is: ONE HUNDRED A DOLLAR, ONE HUNDR DOLLAR, OF ONE HUNDRED DOLLAR This is simply the result of careless work in punching the letters upon the unstruck planchets, and it would be absurd to term such specimens varieties, since a planchet thus bungled is liable to occur impressed with any of the numerous dies.

The first attempt at classification of the cents of 1794 was the work of Dr. Edward Maris, of Philadelphia, appearing in the form of a small pamphlet some eighteen years ago. In connection with his description Dr. Maris employed certain names to designate the varieties, which, although often absurd and highly confusing, have become so firmly attached to the different cents of this year as to render it inadvisible to omit them. There are thirty of these names, which we tabulate in accordance with the numbers of Dr. Maris' list, as follows:

1.	1793 Head.	14.	Abrupt Hair.	32.	Shielded Hair
2.	Double Chin.	15.	Separated Date.	34.	The Plicæ.
3.	Sans Milling.	17.	The Ornate.	36.	The Plicæ.
4.	Tilted 4.	18.	Venus Marina.	37.	The Plicæ.
5.	Young Head.	20.	Fallen 4.	38.	Roman Plica.
6.	The Coquette.	21.	Short Bust.	39.	1795 Head.
7.	Crooked 7.	23.	Patagonian.	41.	Egeria.
10.	Pyramidal Head.	26.	Amiable Face.	42.	Trephined Head.
11.	Many Haired.	28.	Large Planchet.	43.	Crowded Date.
12.	Scarred Head.	29.	Marred Field.	44.	Diana.
13.	Standless 4.	31.	Distant 1.		

The measurement figures which we shall have occasion to employ, refer to the American scale of $\frac{1}{16}$ of an inch to a size. In conclusion let us say that the cents of 1794 in ordinary condition are not of great rarity. Proof or uncirculated specimens, however, invariably command a high price. ⁑

No. 18.—1793 *Head.*—Obv. Head of Liberty to left, with the cap upon the short pole behind. Above the head, LIBERTY In ex., 1794 Date straight, measuring 5 horizontally. The date stands high and close to the bust; the 4 is blunt at the top and almost touches the bust.

Rev.—*Rev. A.*—UNITED STATES OF AMERICA Within a wreath of laurel leaves and berries, tied at the base with a ribbon, ONE | CENT Below the wreath, between the pendant ends of the ribbon, $\frac{1}{100}$ A minute dot (the compass mark) between the E and N of CENT being nearest the N. The top of the N joins the top of the E of ONE. Inclination of wreath stems toward each other, 94° Length of stems from point of union to terminus, right stem : 3½ ; left stem: 3¾. Maris, No. 1. R^{2}.

Such is the type of the cent of 1794. We shall not repeat the description, but treat only of differing points.

No. 19.—*Double Chin.*—Obv. Head very similar to last, the hair somewhat shorter, profile fine and the chin slightly double [not accurately depicted in illustration]. The word LIBERTY is closer to the milling than to the hair. Figures of date are regular and further removed from bust than on No. 18.

Rev.—*Rev. A.*—Maris No. 2. R^{1}.

No. 20.

Rev. B.

No. 20.—*Double Chin.*—Obv. Same as No. 19.

Rev.—*Rev. B.*—ONE CENT stands high in wreath. The dividing line of fraction is nearest denominator. A M of AMERICA are widely separated. A slight crack extends from milling between M and E of AMERICA to T of CENT. Inclination of wreath stems, 104°. Length from point of union of stems to terminus, right stem : 3½ ; left stem : 2¾. This reverse is not mentioned by Maris. R^{2}.

No. 21.—*Sans Milling.*—Obv. The date is long. The staff broadens and presents a flat appearance at the end. The word LIBERTY is widely spaced. The milling is weak and on some specimens does not appear at all. It is probable that Dr. Maris examined a worn specimen—hence the name.

Rev.—*Rev. A.*—Maris, No. 3. R^{2}.

No. 22.—*Tilted 4.*—Obv. The head presents a facial expression very similar to No. 18. The staff is thick and close to the bust. Length of date, 5½ The figures 1, 7 and 9 are of uniform size and evenly spaced,

No. 22.

while the 4 is closer to the 9, below the line of its fellows and is tilted slightly to the right. Distance between top of 4 and bust, $\frac{4}{8}$.

Rev.—*Rev. B.*—Maris, No. 4. R[1].

No. 23. Rev. C.

No. 23.—*Young Head.*—Obv. Presents one of the best designs of the series. The facial expression is calm and dignified, the hair close and waving. The lettering is large and irregular, the R being slightly above the upper line and immediately over the apex of the forehead. A crack in the die extends through E to the top of the head. The date is curved and the figures irregularly spaced, the 7 and 9 being very close; the 4 touches the bust (not so depicted in the illustration).

Rev.—*Rev. C.*—The word STATES is unevenly spaced, the first S being distant from the T. The U and N of UNITED almost touch each other at the top; the D is slightly below the upper line and very close to the E. The wreath joins at top and the right pendant end of the ribbon nearly touches the last cipher of the denominator. Inclination of wreath stem, 100°. Length from point of union of stems to terminus; right stem: $2\frac{1}{2}$; left stem: $3\frac{1}{4}$. Maris, No. 5. R[1].

No. 24.—*Young Head.*—Obv. Same as No. 23.

Rev.—*Rev. D.*—Similar to No. 23, but has between the points of the milling a circle of 87 (?) minute stars. R[8].

No. 25.—*Young Head.*—Obv. Same as No. 23.

Rev.—*Rev. E.*—Differs from reverse of No. 23 in the wreath which is *open* at the top and has six berries on each branch. R[6].

No. 26.

No. 26.—*Coquette.*—Obv. The letter L of LIBERTY touches the I and almost touches the cap. The point where the first three locks become separated below the ear is the centre of an arc formed on the neck by the wavy hair.

Rev.—*Rev. C.*—Maris, No. 6. R[4].

No. 27.

No. 27.—*Crooked* 7.—Obv. The marked peculiarity of this obverse lies in the date. The 1 and 4 touch the hair and bust, respectively. The 7 is disproportionately large, the stem being being strongly inclined to the left. The letter R of LIBERTY is very close to the hair, the lower curve blending with the stand of the T (not represented in the illustration).

Rev.—*Rev. C.*—Maris, No. 7. R[1].

No. 28.—*Crooked* 7.—Obv. Same as No. 27.

Rev.—*Rev. F.*—The letters T and A of STATES are joined at the bottom. The right perpendicular stroke of the N of ONE is somewhat longer at the lower end than the left. Inclination of wreath stems, 120°. Length of stems from point of union to terminus, right stem: 3; left stem: 3. Maris, No. 7. R[1].

No. 29.—*Crooked* 7.—Obv. Same as No. 27.

Rev.—*Rev. G.*—The spacing of the word STATES is very irregular and the letters uneven. The A is abnormally large and rises above the upper line of the other letters, being also very close to the first T. The first T is below the upper line. The E of ONE is crooked, and tilts forward, being also above the upper line of the O and N. The T of CENT is above the upper line of the CEN. Maris, No. 7. R[1].

The *Crooked* 7 cents are found perfect and with both obverse and reverse dies cracked across.

No. 30.

No. 30.—*Pyramidal Head.*—Obv. The letter L of LIBERTY closely approaches the cap, and the R the hair. The forehead is high and receding—this probably suggested the name—its apex being directly beneath the letter R. The date is close and curved. The 1 touches the hair (not so represented in the illustration), the 4 is sharp and almost touches the bust (distance one-half millimeter).

Rev.—*Rev. H.*—On this reverse ONE | CENT is high in the wreath, the distance between the letter C and the nearest leaf being 1. The words STATES and AMERICA are irregularly spaced, the letters T and M being out of position. The branches of the wreath have 7 berries each; the two lower berries on the left touch the ribbon. Inclination of wreath stems, 118°. Length from point of union of stems to terminus, right stem: 2¼; left stem: 2½. The fraction measures 3 horizontally and is much below the wreath. The numerator and the figure 1 in the denominator are very close to the dividing line, the ciphers being somewhat lower. Maris, No. 10. R[1].

No. 31.

No. 31.—*Many-Haired.*—Obv. The hair is thick, the face well designed and of pleasing expression; the tip of the nose is distant 3 from the stand of the letter Y of LIBERTY. The letters of LIBERTY are uneven, the R being slightly above the upper line. The whole touches the milling. The date is bold and curved, and measures 5½ horizontally. The figure 1 touches the hair.

Rev.—*Rev. I.*—There are 7 berries on each branch of the wreath. The dash of the fraction is inclined downward, to right. The last cipher is very close to the milling. Inclination of wreath stems, 119°. Length of stems from point of union to terminus, right stem: 2¾; left stem: 2½. Maris, No. 11. R[1].

No. 32.

No. 32.—*Scarred Head.*—Obv. This variety is easily distinguished by a depression in the hair just below the ear. The word LIBERTY is evenly spaced and equally distant from cap, head and milling. The lower curl is long and points toward the top of the 1 in date. The date is irregular, the figure 7 being shorter than its fellows and the 4 blunt and badly formed; the 1 is close to the hair.

Rev.—*Rev. J.*—The letter C of CENT is disproportionately small. The numerator and the figure 1 in denominator of fraction touch the dividing line. Inclination of wreath stems, 110°. Length of stems from point of union to terminus, right stem: 3; left stem: 3. Maris, No. 12. R^1.

No. 33.

No. 33.—*Standless 4.*—Obv. The letters of the word LIBERTY are irregular and close to the milling. The date is small and close and placed equally distant from bust, hair and milling. The figure 4 lacks the horizontal stand. Specimens from this die show two cracks; one extending from a point near the ear, downward across the pole at its end; the other from the milling to the right of the letter R of LIBERTY downward to the nose (not represented in the illustration).

Rev.—*Rev. K.*—The letter M of AMERICA is smaller than its fellows and the R disproportionately large. Inclination of wreath stems, 112°. Length of stems from point of union to terminus, right stem: 3; left stem: 3. Maris, No. 13. R^2.

No. 34.—*Abrupt Hair.*—Obv. Two locks of hair pass near the cap and terminate abruptly. The ends of the two locks immediately below the cap are disconnected from the rest. The word LIBERTY is regular and close to the milling. The date is more evenly spaced than is represented in our illustration, is curved and very close to the milling.

No. 34.

Rev.—*Rev. L.*—This die presents two cracks. One extending from the milling between the A and second T of STATES, curves downward and merges with the O, of ONE. The other passes through D of UNITED, to the top of C of CENT; thence curving downward, merges with the N of ONE. Inclination of wreath stems, 130°. Length of stems from point of union to terminus, right stem : 2½ ; left stem : 2½. **Maris**, No. 14. R^2.

No. 35. Rev. M.

No. 35.—*Separated Date.*—Obv. The word LIBERTY is evenly spaced and very close to the milling; the letter T is a trifle lower than its follows. The date is large, widely separated and made up of uneven figures. The 1 is nearer the milling than the hair; the 7 has a short downward stroke; the 9 is badly formed, closer to the 4 than to the 7 and touches the milling; the 4 stands midway between milling and bust. The hair is lightly cut, which gives it a scanty appearance. The line from the tip of the nose to the apex of the head is less abrupt than in No. 34.

Rev.—*Rev. M.*—Presents a die-crack extending from the milling through the E of STATES to the outermost leaf of the left branch of the wreath, which it touches; thence, on some specimens, across the E of ONE to the right branch. Other specimens still show a crack through the first S of STATES extending toward the centre of the planchet. Inclination of wreath stems, 120°. Length of stems from point of union to terminus, right stem: $2\frac{3}{4}$; left stem: 3. From the end of the left stem to the extreme left of the ribbon bow is 3. Maris, No. 15. R[1].

No. 36.—*Separated Date.*—Obv. Same as No. 35.

Rev.—*Rev. N.*—Distance from end of left stem to extreme left of ribbon bow, 4. Inclination of stems, 113°. Length of stems from point of union to terminus, right stem: 3; left stem: $3\frac{1}{4}$. Maris, No. 19. R[1].

No. 37.—*The Ornate.*—Obv. The facial expression is calm and dignified. The lower curl of the hair points directly to the top of 1 in date. The letters of LIBERTY are regularly formed and widely spaced, being close to the milling and equally distant from head and cap. From the tip of chin to the lowest point of L is 11. The date is widely spaced and measures 6 in width.

No. 37.

Rev.—*Rev. O.*—The E of ONE and the T of CENT are smaller than the other letters. The C and A of AMERICA approach each other closely. Inclination of wreath stems, 100°. Length of stems from point of union to terminus, right stem: 3; left stem: 3. Maris, No. 17. R.[1]

No. 38.—*The Ornate.*—Obv. Same as No. 37.

Rev.—*Rev. P.*—The E of ONE is above, and the C of CENT, below the line of the other letters. The wreath is lightly struck and the branches much twisted and very irregular. The right pendant end of the ribbon touches the milling. Inclination of wreath stems,

102°. Length of stems from point of union to terminus, right stem 3; left stem: 3½. Maris, No. 25. R².

No. 39.

No. 39.—*Venus Marina.*—Obv. The head presents perhaps the most beautiful facial expression of the series and fully justifies its name. The hair is thick and long and the cap approaches very close to the milling. The letters of LIBERTY are evenly spaced and near the milling, which has a slight defect between the L and I The date is regular and measures 5¾ in width.

Rev.—*Rev. Q.*—Similar to *Rev. O*, AMERICA being evenly spaced. A die-crack extends from the first S of STATES toward the centre of the planchet. The dividing line of the fraction measures 2¼. Inclination of wreath stems, 124°. Length of stems from point of union to terminus, right stem: 3; left stem: 3. Maris, No. 18. R¹.

No. 40.—*Venus Marina.*—Obv. Similar to No. 39. The die shows a crack extending through the L of LIBERTY in a curved line across the cap.

Rev.—*Rev. R.*—One berry only upon the left branch of the wreath opposite the top of the ribbon bow. The bow is much out of place. Inclination of wreath stems, 125°. Length of stems from point of union to terminus, right stem: 2¾; left stem: 2¾. Maris, No. 19. R¹.

No. 41.—*Fallen 4.*—Obv. The face is bold and striking. The word LIBERTY is unevenly spaced, the B and E being closer than the I and B or the E and R; each letter touches the milling; the letter L is distant from the cap. The date is irregularly spaced; the figures 179 are on a line, but the 4, which touches the 9, presents the appearance of having fallen slightly below.

No. 41.

Rev.—*Rev. S.*—The dividing line of the fraction touches the right pendant ribbon end. Inclination of wreath stems, 101°. Length of stems from point of union to terminus, right stem : 3¼ ; left stem : 3¼. Maris, No. 20. R[1].

No. 42.

No. 42.—*Short Bust.*—Obv. The facial expression is coarse and not pleasing. The bust line is slightly rounded and shorter than on the other varieties of this date. The word LIBERTY is close, irregular and stands about midway between hair and milling. The date is close and irregularly spaced, the figures 7 and 9 almost touch. The figure 1 almost touches the hair and the 4 touches the bust. A die-crack extends from the left of the cap through the hair, thence to the left of date to the milling.

Rev.—*Rev. T.*—A die-crack shows itself at the milling between the words STATES and OF, extending to the N of ONE. Inclination of wreath stems, 130°. Length of stems from point of union to terminus, right stem : 2½ ; left stem : 3. Maris, No. 21. R[1].

No. 43.—*Short Bust.*—Obv. Same as No. 42.

Rev.—*Rev. U.*—A die-crack shows itself at U of UNITED, passes through C of CENT and O of ONE to the wreath. Inclination of wreath stems, 135°. Length of stems from point of union to terminus, right stem: 2½; left stem: 2½. Maris, No. 22. R[1].

No. 44.

No. 44.—*Patagonian*—Obv. The head is large and handsome, the face highly expressive, the depression between the chin and lip unusually deep. The word LIBERTY is evenly spaced and is considerably below the milling; the R almost touches the hair. The top of the cap is broad, measuring 1¾ and touches the milling. The staff touches the milling. The distance from the foot of R of LIBERTY to the top of the figure 1 of the date is 12. The figure 1 of the date touches the hair and the 4 the bust. The 7 and 9 are very close to each other.

Rev.—*Rev. V.*—The letter E of ONE is above the line of its fellows. Inclination of wreath stems, 135°. Length of stems from point of union to terminus, right stem: 2; left stem: 2½; Maris, No. 23. R[1].

No. 45.—*Patagonian.*—Obv. Same as No. 44.

Rev.—*Rev. W.*—The letters composing the word ONE are on a line. Inclination of wreath stems, 128°. Length of stems from point of union to terminus, right stem: 2½; left stem: 3. Maris, No. 24. R[1]

No. 46.

No. 46.—*Amiable Face.*—Obv. Our illustration does not fairly represent the facial expression, which is decidedly amiable, and fully bears out the name. There is a small disconnected lock of hair at a distance of 2½ below the cap. The distance from the ear to the lowest point of the letter Y of LIBERTY is 6. The word LIBERTY is irregular and nearer the milling than the head. The date is likewise irregular, but the figures 7 and 9 are not as close as represented in our illustration. The 7 is smaller than the other figures; the 1 stands considerably below the 7; the 4 is very close to the bust.

Rev.—*Rev. P.*—Maris, No. 26. R¹. This variety occurs on large and small planchets.

No. 47.—*Amiable Face.*—Obv. Same as No. 46.

Rev.—*Rev. X.*—The ribbon knot is particularly prominent; the dividing line of fraction measures 3. Inclination of wreath stems: 124°. Length of stems from point of union to terminus, right stem, 2¾; left stem: 2⅞. Maris, No. 27. R¹.

No. 48.

No. 48.—*Large Planchet.*—Obv. Head not unhandsome; features clear and well defined. Distance from the top of the figure 1 of the date to the tip of the nose is 11. The word LIBERTY is even and near the milling. The letters L and R are equally distant from cap and hair. The date is regular and measures 5 in length.

Rev.—*Rev. Y.*—The left branch of the wreath bears six large and two small berries, the latter being divided by the last leaf. The letters T and A of STATES almost touch at base. Inclination of wreath stems, 119°. Length of stems from point of union to terminus, right stem: 2½; left stem: 2½. Maris, No. 28. R¹. This variety is usually found struck upon large planchets.

No. 49.—*Marred Field.*—Obv. This obverse is identical with No. 46, the Amiable Face, but has behind the head the peculiar mark described as a detached lock of hair, and a slight blemish on the smooth surface of the field.

Rev.—*Rev. X.* Maris, No. 29. R[1].

No. 50.—*Marred Field.*—Obv. Same as No. 49.

Rev.—*Rev. Z.*—The top of the slanting stroke of the N of UNITED is unusually long. A die-crack shows itself above U of UNITED, extending to the N. Another crack appears crossing the letter D. Dividing line of fraction measures 2¼. Inclination of wreath stems, 130°. Length of stems from point of union to terminus, right stem: 2½; left stem: 2½. Maris, No. 30. R[1].

No. 51.—*Distant* 1.—Obv. The head is marked by the third and fifth locks of hair being of greater length than the others, also by the peculiarity of the pole, which appears to terminate at the bust with a separate stick attached beneath, extending to the milled border. This peculiarity exists in no other obverse of the cents of 1794. The word LIBERTY is somewhat uneven, the letter L is near the cap. The date is curved, the figure 1 being at an unusual distance from the 7, and the 4 showing but faint traces of a stand. The distance from the top of the figure 1 to the tip of the nose is 11; from the lower left point of the figure 1 to the end of the pole (the apparent termination at the bust is signified) is 8¾.

Rev.—*Rev. AA.*—The letter E of AMERICA is smaller than its fellows. The letter C of CENT is below the line of the remaining letters of the word. The distance from the upper left hand point of the last T of STATES to the upper right hand point of F in OF is 9½. The dividing line of the fraction measures 1¾. Inclination of wreath stems, 107°. Length of stems from point of union of terminus, right stem: 3; left stem: 3. Maris, No. 31. R[3].

No. 52.—*Shielded Hair.*—Obv. The facial expression is particularly handsome, the hair thick and wavy. The letters of the word LIBERTY are somewhat irregular; the L is near the cap and the R near the hair. The date is curved; the figure 1 touches the hair (not so depicted in the illustration) and the 4 the bust. A die-crack extends

No. 52.

from bust to milling, passing through 9 in the date. The milled border in this variety is unusually wide on the left and at the base of the planchet.

Rev.—*Rev. BB.*—Bears a close resemblance to *Rev. Z.* There is a die-crack extending through the last S of STATES to the N of ONE; and again through the last A of AMERICA to the bow. Inclination of wreath stems 130°. Length of stems from point of union to terminus, right stem: 2¼: left stem: 2¼. Maris, No. 32. R¹.

No. 53.—*Shielded Hair.*—Obv. Same as No. 52.

Rev.—*Rev. CC.*—The fraction shows no dividing line. A die-crack extends through the letter D of UNITED. Inclination of wreath stems, 125°. Length of stems from point of union to terminus, right stem: 3; left stem: 2½. R¹.

No. 54.

No. 54.—*Plica, No.* 1.—Obv. The hair presents a twisted, matted appearance—hence the name (from *plico*, to twist, to fold). The letters of the word LIBERTY are uneven, the L is very close to the cap. From the extreme end of the bust to the lowest point of the letter Y the distance is 9. A line drawn from the chin to the back of the head in the direction of the letter L of LIBERTY will be found to measure 8¾. The figure 7 of the date has a long stem which touches the milled border.

Rev.—*Rev. DD.*—The letter A of STATES almost touches the first T. A slight elevation in the field has the appearance of an interrupted continuation of the right ribbon end and extends almost to the milling. Length of the dividing line of fraction is 2. Inclination of wreath stems, 123°. Length of stems from point of union to terminus, right stem: 2$\frac{3}{5}$; left stem: 2½. Maris, No. 34. R[1].

No. 55.

No. 55.—*Plica No. 2.*—Obv. This obverse is from the same die as No. 54, but of later execution, presenting a crack extending across the bust parallel with the pole. (The apparent crack across the letter T of LIBERTY depicted in our illustration is inaccurate. The engraver made use of a specimen which had been subjected to a blow). There is also a small break in the milled border, damaging the figure 4 in such a manner that another seems to have been substituted and placed nearer the bust.

Rev.—*Rev. EE.*—A faint die-crack shows itself, extending from the letter N of ONE through E of CENT. Inclination of wreath stems, 125°. Length of stems from point of union to terminus, right stem: 2$\frac{1}{2}$; left stem: 2. Maris, No. 35. R[1].

No. 56.—*Plica No. 3.*—Obv. Head very similar to Plicæ Nos. 1 and 2. The hair curls sharply toward the top of the figure 1. The word LIBERTY is widely spaced except between L and I. A die-crack extends from the milling between the letters T and Y of LIBERTY across the head. The figures of the date are regular and widely spaced.

Rev.—*Rev. FF.*—The letters S and first T of STATES are above the line of their fellows. The last A of AMERICA is likewise out of position.

No. 56.

Inclination of wreath stems, 114°. Length of stems from point of union to terminus, right stem: 3⅛; left stem: 3. Maris, No. 36. R[1].

No. 57.—*Plica No. 4.*—Obv. Similar to No. 56, but the L of LIBERTY is nearer the cap. The lowest lock of hair, also, describes a greater arch than on No. 56, and is not so broad.

Rev.—*Rev. FF.*—Not mentioned by Maris. R[1].

No. 58.—*Roman Plica.*—Obv. The head is very similar to those of the Plicæ (Nos. 54, 55, 56 and 57), but the facial expression is sterner. The lowest lock of hair corresponds closely with No. 57. The date is more widely spaced than is the case with the Plicæ.

Rev.—*Rev. AA.*—Maris, No. 38. R[1].

No. 59.

No. 59.—1795 *Head.*—Obv. The head corresponds in every particular to that of the 1795 cent. The lowest curl curves but slightly, ending in an abrupt manner, similar to the other locks. The letter L of LIBERTY touches the cap and the R and T are close to the head. The date is widely spaced, the figure 9 being below the line of its fellows.

Rev.—*Rev. GG.*—The letters composing the word CENT are very irregular. Inclination of wreath stems, 103°. Length of stems from point of union to terminus, right stem: 3; left stem: 3. Maris, No. 39. R^3.

No. 60.—*Many-Haired.*—Obv. Same as No. 31.

Rev.—*Rev. HH.*—Differs from *Rev. I* in having but *six* berries on left branch of the wreath. Inclination of wreath stems, 120°. Length of stems from point of union to terminus, right stem: 2¼; left stem: 2¼. Maris, No. 40. R^3.

No. 61.—*Egeria.*—Obv. Similar to No. 37. The figure 7 of the date stands in a different relative position to the 1; the 4 is nearer the bust. There are but *seven* ends to the locks of hair instead of eight, as in No. 37.

Rev.—*Rev. O.*—Maris, No. 41. R^3.

No. 62.—*Trephined Head.*—Obv. The facial expression is bold and striking. There is a depression in the head just below the point of union with the cap, a peculiarity not found on any other variety. The lowest lock of hair is unusually thick. The letters of the word LIBERTY are regular and evenly spaced. The date measures 5 in width. A large fragment broken from the die at the milled border on the left, furnishes another marked distinguishing feature of this variety.

Rev.—*Rev. V.*—Maris, No. 42. R^1.

No. 63.—*Crowded Date.*—Obv. The head presents no marked distinguishing feature. The letter L of the word LIBERTY is distant ⅝ from the cap; the R 1¼ from the head. The pole has an unusually broad end. The date is near the bust, the figure 4 touching it. Length of date, 5½.

Rev.—*Rev. II.*—The left branch of the wreath has but a single berry which is opposite the ribbon bow, as on *Rev. R.* The bow in this instance is, however, in its proper position. Inclination of wreath stems, 127°. Length of stems from point of union to terminus, right stem: 2¾; left stem: 2½. Maris, No. 43. R^3.

No. 64.—*Diana.*—Obv. The hair ends in seven long wavy points. The word LIBERTY is uneven, the R touching the border and above the line of its fellows. Distance from the extreme point of the bust to the end of the lowest curl is 8½, which is greater than on any other variety. A die-crack extends from the border through the right lower arm of the letter E of LIBERTY to a point just below the ear. The date is separated in a manner similar to No. 35, the figure 7 being at a greater distance from the 1 than is the case with that variety, and slants more to the right.

Rev.—*Rev. JJ.*—The last S in the word STATES is above the line of its fellows. Inclination of wreath stems, 120°. Length of stems from point of union to terminus, right stem: 2; left stem: 2¼. Maris, No. 44. R³.

No. 65.—*Double Chin.*—Obv. Same as No. 20.

Rev.—*Rev. B.*—R³.

With No. 65 our enumeration of the varieties of the cents of 1794 closes. It is in all respects the most remarkable group of the series, no other year from 1793 down to the present offering so large a number of differing dies. It will be observed by those who compare our enumeration with former lists of the cents of 1794, that we have rejected several numbers entirely. Our desire has been to adhere strictly to *actual* varieties, and the collector may rely upon it that in the present list are to be found all worthy of a place.

1795.

The cents of the year 1795 bear a close general resemblance to those of the preceding year. The liberty cap is retained and those issued early in the year were struck upon thick planchets with the edge inscription: ONE HUNDRED FOR A DOLLAR. Later the thin planchet was adopted and the edge inscription dropped. The borders are milled. Upon some specimens blunders in the edge inscriptions appear, as upon the cents of 1794. We shall not enumerate these blunders since they can in no sense be termed varieties, the edges of the planchets being lettered, as has already been stated, previous to the striking of the cent; hence the possible occurrence of the error upon any variety, and the impossibility of giving to any blundered specimen a number or place.

No. 66.

Rev. A.

No. 66.—Obv. Head in all respects similar to that upon the cents of 1794. The word LIBERTY is irregular, the letters LIBE being a little lower than the RTY The length of the word is 11. The L is very close to the cap but does not actually touch it, as represented in our illustration. The letter T is directly opposite the forelock. The date is widely spaced and measures 5½. The figure 5 merges with the bust.

Rev.—*Rev. A.*—Design and legend the same as upon the cents of 1794. ONE CENT stands high within the wreath. The right stem of wreath points directly toward the right foot of the letter A of AMERICA The dividing line of the fraction is short, measuring but 1½.

Edge.—ONE HUNDRED FOR A DOLLAR. Struck upon a thick planchet. R^2.

No. 67.—Obv. Head closely resembles No. 66. The word LIBERTY is slightly irregular. The letter L is distant ½ from cap. The forelock points to the space between R and T. The date is large and widely spaced, the figure 1 being under the hair, while the 5 merges with the bust. The distance from the chin to the highest point of the letter Y of LIBERTY is 6½.

Rev.—*Rev. B.*—ONE CENT stands about in the centre of the wreath. Upon either side of the bow, below the loops, is a berry. The right branch of the wreath, unlike any other specimen of this date, terminates in two leaves. The right stem points to the centre of the letter A of AMERICA. The dividing line of the fraction measures 1¾.

Edge.—ONE HUNDRED FOR A DOLLAR. Struck upon a thick planchet. R^2.

No. 68.

Rev. C.

No. 68.—Obv. Same as No. 67.

Rev.—*Rev. C.*—The branches of the wreath present a wavy appearance. There is a berry near the left loop of the bow, but none near the right. The dividing line of the fraction touches all the figures. The distance from the centre of knot to the numerator is 2. The denominator almost touches the milled border.

Edge.—ONE HUNDRED FOR A DOLLAR Struck upon a thick planchet. R^2.

No. 69.—Obv. Same as No. 66.

Rev.—*Rev. D.*—The branches of the wreath are thick, with 20 leaves upon the right and 21 upon the left branch. The wreath itself describes a complete circle. The legend is very close to the wreath. The right wreath stem points to the right of the letter A of AMERICA. The border milling is finer than upon other reverse varieties of the cents of this year, and bears a marked resemblance to the reverses of the cents of 1796.

Edge.—Plain. Struck upon a thin planchet. R^2. Specimens of this cent are to be found with a die-crack upon the obverse, beginning at the shoulder above the date and extending upward through the cap to the border.

No. 70.—Obv. The facial expression is calm and dignified and of much better execution from an artistic standpoint than upon the preceding numbers. The pole is thicker and longer than upon other varieties and touches the milled border. The letters of the word LIBERTY are very close and the word but slightly curved, the extreme measurement being 9½. The letter L is distant ¾ from the cap. The forelock points between the letters T and Y. The distance from the

No. 70.

chin to the highest point of the letter Y is $7\frac{3}{4}$. The date is bold and regular; the figures 1 and 7 are distant from the bust. The figure 5 just touches bust (not so represented in our illustration) the full curve of the upper stroke being visible. Extreme measurement of date is $4\frac{3}{4}$.

Rev.—*Rev. E.*—ONE CENT occupies a central position within the wreath. There are 3 berries upon the right branch of the wreath, and 4 on the left. To the left of the centre of the letter C of CENT two leaves terminate. There is a berry opposite the loop of the left bow, but none on the right. The wreath stems are long, that on the right almost touching the letter A of AMERICA, while the left stem stands in the same relative position to the letter U of UNITED. The length of the dividing line of the fraction is 2.

Edge.—Plain. Struck upon a thin planchet. R[1].

THE JEFFERSON HEAD CENT.

The Jefferson Head.—This obverse differs entirely from all other varieties of the Liberty Cap cents, as will be seen by the illustration. The facial expression is coarse, the hair long and stiff; the usual hair [illegible] 1 [illegible] 2 5 6 7

[illegible]-68, [illegible] "Hyphen, 60, 69, [illegible], [illegible]", [illegible]

The "rounded edge," [illegible] [illegible] of '76, G-5(6), [illegible]

[illegible] [illegible] [illegible] the [illegible] "[illegible]" [illegible] [illegible]

[illegible] as a [illegible] [illegible], not [illegible] [illegible]

features of the [illegible] and [illegible]. [illegible]

[illegible] tried to pick out some [illegible] of [illegible] that would tie up with '94 but failed. [illegible] [illegible] [illegible] [illegible] [illegible] coming [illegible] [illegible] "queer," but G-I and K have the other [illegible] of the "rounded edge."

The [illegible] of the Cap in '95 will [illegible] [illegible] [illegible] to 11-6-7-8 ~~[illegible]~~ but the [illegible] [illegible] at right bottom is [illegible] [illegible]. [illegible] [illegible] new [illegible] [illegible] the [illegible] [illegible] [illegible] [illegible] [illegible] out in ~~[illegible]~~ '95 [illegible] [illegible] [illegible] [illegible] [illegible] [illegible] [illegible] [illegible] [illegible] [illegible] [illegible] [illegible] [illegible] [illegible].

[illegible] [illegible]. [illegible], the [illegible] [illegible] [illegible] [illegible] [illegible] [illegible] [illegible] [illegible] [illegible] [illegible] single [illegible] [illegible] [illegible] [illegible] [illegible] the [illegible] cap of '96. [illegible] [illegible] [illegible] [illegible] [illegible] [illegible] [illegible] [illegible] [illegible] [illegible] [illegible] [illegible] [illegible] [illegible] [illegible] [illegible] [illegible] [illegible]

[illegible] D G [illegible] come ahead of C [illegible]
[illegible]

1795
Milled
Edge.
2
[illegible]

McGirk's Milled edge 1795. His #6A
[illegible] (In Coll. S.H.C.) (A.N.S. 2/37.)

[illegible] His. Rev G-5 [illegible] before break under E of UNITED.

ribbon above the forehead is lacking and the pole is thin and short. The letters of the word LIBERTY are regular and widely spaced, and are much heavier than upon other varieties. The extreme measurement of the word is 11, the letter L being 1 distant from the cap while the forelock points to the letter R. The cap is much smaller than upon other varieties, its extreme length being 5⅛, extreme width 4. The date is small and cramped, the figures are thin and irregular and present the appearance of having been engraved. Extreme measurement of date, 4½. Distance from the figure 1 to the point of the bust, 6¼.

Rev.—The reverse of this cent differs from all others of the series, as does the obverse. The letters of the legend are coarse and heavy. The wreath is badly executed; the leaves in many instances being entirely without stems, while in others the stems are unusually long. The ribbon bow is unusual also in being tied in three loops and the fraction is very large.

Edge.—Plain. Struck upon a thick planchet. *A counterfeit.* X

Beyond all question the Jefferson Head cent of 1795 is a counterfeit. One glance at our illustration in comparison with the others of the Liberty Cap series should be quite sufficient to show any person open to conviction that it never emanated from the United States mint.

As we cannot include it in our list, we have omitted to number the Jefferson Head cent, and for the further enlightenment of the reader would call his attention to the following, which appeared in the COIN COLLECTOR'S JOURNAL, Vol, V., page 35:

"This so-called 'Jefferson Head' cent was probably so named for the same reason as the Guinea pigs, because they are not pigs and do not come from Guinea. The portrait on the piece does not resemble Jefferson, nor did he have aught to do with the issue, while last, but not least, *it is not a cent*, but undoubtedly a counterfeit of the cent of 1795, struck somewhere about the year 1803. The workmanship and style of every portion of this piece show that the dies were never executed at the United States mint. The hair alone should be sufficient to condemn it, since no artist employed in the mint from its first establishment would have engraved such a stiff unnatural mass while having for models the beautiful wavy locks which adorn the earlier coins. The figures and letters are totally unlike any used on the cents. The figures of the fraction are the size of those of the cent of 1803. The wreath, with its lobster-claw leaves and three-looped bow, furnishes further evidence of the inexpert tool of an imitator, who had before him different types of cents and engraved the least difficult part of each. The short and narrow serrated border on the reverse is unlike any used in 1795, while the absence of border ornamentation on the obverse, even on the best specimens, would seem to indicate that a worn cent had been copied."

1796.

The cents of 1796 are divided into two distinct series. Those of the first series in every way resemble the Liberty Cap cents of 1793, 1794 and 1795. The second series marks an entire change of obverse and the adoption of a new head of Liberty, which continued in use until the year 1808. This head of Liberty has been differently styled the "Fillet Head" and the "Draped Bust." The latter term is certainly to be preferred. The reverse dies of the cents of this year were of the same general design of those preceding it. The borders of the cents of 1796 are generally found milled, the planchets thin, and the edges always plain.

FIRST SERIES.

No. 71.

Rev A.

No. 71.—Obv. The head presents the same general appearance as those preceding. The hair is thin; the staff touches the bust and extends almost to the milling. The letter L of LIBERTY touches the cap; the apex of the forehead is between the T and Y. The date is curved and more evenly spaced than is represented in our illustration. The figure 6 is very close to the bust, but does not touch. A few of the measurements are: Length of pole, 3¼; width of date, ⅘; distance from upper left hand corner of 7 to the point of bust, 5½.

Rev.—*Rev. A.*—The word CENT is very low within the wreath, and is distant 1½ from ONE. There are 4 berries on the right branch of the wreath and 5 on the left. The A and M of AMERICA are joined at the feet. The lower leaf on the right branch of the wreath points between the feet of the terminal A (not so represented in our illustration). The dividing line of fraction is slightly curved and the final 0 in the denominator higher than the other figures. R[1].

No. 72.—Obv. Same as No. 71.

Rev.—*Rev. B.*—The letters of the word CENT are irregular, the T being inclined slightly to the right and its top below the line of its fellows. Distance between ONE and CENT is 1. The lowest leaf on the right branch of the wreath points to the left foot of the terminal A of AMERICA; another leaf touches the F in OF. There are 5 berries on each branch. The letters M and R of AMERICA touch at the feet. R[1].

No. 73.—Obv. Distance from tip of nose to the nearest point of the letter Y of LIBERTY is 2¾. The staff is thicker between the head and cap than at the projecting end. The letter L of LIBERTY does not touch the cap. The date is long, its extreme measurement being 5, while the distance from the upper right hand corner of the figure 7 to the point of the bust is 6¼. Distance from the figure 1 to the hair, ½; from the figure 6 to the bust, ¾.

Rev.—*Rev. B.* R[1].

No. 74.—Obv. Same as No. 73.

Rev.—*Rev. C.*—Distance between the words ONE and CENT, 1. The letter T of CENT is inclined slightly to the right. There are 20 leaves on the right branch of the wreath and 21 on the left, principally in groups of three, with 5 berries on either branch. The lowest of a group of three leaves on the left branch touches the base of the letter C of CENT. The lowest leaf on the right branch touches the right foot of the letter A of AMERICA, while the lowest leaf on the left branch points toward U of UNITED, The dividing line of the fraction is straight and the full width of the denominator. R[1].

No. 75.—Obv. Same as No. 73.

Rev.—*Rev. D.*—The letters AME are connected at the feet. The lowest leaf on the left branch of the wreath almost touches the letter U of UNITED. The highest leaves on both branches terminate directly beneath the letter E of STATES. Length of right wreath stem, 2¼. R[4].

No. 76.—Obv. Same as No. 73.

Rev.—*Rev. E.*—The letters A and M of AMERICA are connected at the feet. The lowest leaf on the left branch of the wreath points toward the space between the letters U and N of UNITED. Length of wreath stems from point of union to terminus, 3. R[1].

No. 77.—Obv. The staff is thin near the neck and broad at the lower end. Extending from the nose to the milling are two parallel lines. The letter L almost touches the cap. *Measurements:* From the tip of nose to the nearest point of the letter Y of LIBERTY, 3¼; length of date, 5½; distance between figure 1 and hair, ½; distance between figure 6 and bust, ½. The figure 7 stands a little higher than the 1. At the 6 a slight die crack appears, extending to the milling; and the surface of the planchet is raised where the pole meets the neck. On some specimens these defects are more noticeable than on others.

Rev.—*Rev. F.*—The wreath upon this reverse differs from all others found upon the cents of this series in the arrangement of the lowest leaves on each side which are in groups of two. There are 16 leaves on the right branch and 19 on the left, with 5 berries on each. The lowest leaf on the left branch points toward the letter N of UNITED while that on the right branch points toward the letter C of AMERICA. The inner leaves do not touch the letters C and T of CENT. Length of right wreath stem, 2¼. The figures of the fraction are thick and do not quite touch the dividing line. R[1].

No. 78.—Obv. This obverse closely resembles No. 77. The staff is more distant from the bust, and tapers to a point where it joins with the neck. The letter L of LIBERTY touches the cap. The letter T is not so close to the head as on No. 77. The figure 1 is closer to the hair and the 6 to the bust than on No. 77.

Rev.—*Rev. E.* R[1].

No. 79.—Obv. The staff is very thin and is connected with the point of the bust by a die-crack. The date is a little nearer the bust than on No. 78; the top of the figure 9 is below the 7. *Measurements:* Length of date, 5½; distance from figures 1 to lowest lock of hair, ⅓.

Rev.—*Rev. B.* R[4].

No. 80.—Obv. This obverse is distinguished by the shortness of the staff, which measures but 2¾. The date is widely spaced and curved; the figure 6 touches the bust and the 1 almost touches the hair. The 7 is somewhat lower than the 1.

Rev.—*Rev. E.* R[4].

SECOND SERIES.

No. 81.

No. 81.—Obv. Bust of Liberty to left. The hair is tied back with a ribbon, below which it falls loosely in curling locks about the neck. The bust, of which more is seen than on the cents of the Liberty Cap series, is partially draped. Above the head, LIBERTY In ex., 1796. The date is curved, more evenly spaced than represented in our illustration, and measures 5 in length. The figure 6 stands perfectly upright and is distant ⅓ from the bust.

Rev.—*Rev. G.*—The letters A and M of AMERICA connect at the feet; the E is more distant from the M than upon other reverses. The upper terminal leaves of the wreath are single and point directly at each other but do not touch. There are 17 leaves and 4 berries on the right branch of wreath and 20 leaves and 5 berries on the left. The left stem almost touches the U of UNITED, and the right the A of AMERICA. The lowest leaf on right branch terminates between the letters I and C of AMERICA; another has its tip immediately beneath the O in OF, while an inner leaf touches the foot of the T of CENT. Length of wreath stems from point of union to terminus, 3. Distance between extreme points of stems, 5¾. The figures of the fraction are small; the dividing line almost touches the right ribbon and has an extreme length of 2. R[1]. On some specimens of this number a die-crack appears, extending from the top of the R of AMERICA through the letters ICA.

No. 82.—Obv. Same as No. 81.

Rev.—*Rev. II*—The letters TAT of STATES and AME of AMERICA are connected at their feet. The wreath has 19 leaves on the right branch and 16 on the left, with 5 berries on either branch. The stems are short, measuring 2¼ each, with a dividing space at the extreme ends of 4½, The lowest leaf on the right branch touches the right foot of the letter A of AMERICA. The right branch terminates at the top in two leaves. The fraction stands at a distance of 1¼ below the knot and midway between the pendant ribbon ends. The first 0 is lower than its fellows. Distance between the ribbon ends, 3¾. R[1]. It is a fact worth noting that on all wreaths where the right branch terminates in two leaves above, no berry is found opposite the bow below; while those terminating in a single leaf, in every instance have a berry to the right of the bow.

No. 83.—Obv. Same as No. 81. This obverse when combined with *Rev. I*, shows two die-cracks. One connecting the figure 6 with the bust, the other beginning below the 9, extending through the 7 and 1, thence to the lower curl and the milling.

Rev.—*Rev. I.*—This wreath has 19 leaves and 5 berries on the right branch and 16 leaves and 6 berries on the left. The right branch terminates in two leaves, its lowest leaf being opposite the letter C of AMERICA. The wreath stems are short, but the stems of the berries are all long. The loops of the bow are disconnected from the branches; the right pendant ribbon end approaches very closely to the letter A of AMERICA. Distance between the ribbon ends is 5. The fraction measures 2¾ in length and stands ¾ below the knot; the figures are large and the dividing line measures but 1½. R[1].

No. 84.—Obv. Same as No. 81.

Rev.—*Rev. J.*—This wreath has 18 leaves and 5 berries on the right branch, and 16 leaves and 5 berries on the left. The right branch terminates in 2 leaves, very close to the letter E of STATES. There is but a single leaf at the base of the right branch (other varieties have two) which points toward the letter I of AMERICA. The stems are distant 2¾ from the knot. Distance between the pendant ribbon ends, 4½. The fraction stands a trifle higher than on *Rev. I*; the figures are large. R[4].

No. 85. Rev. K.

G-3

No. 85.—Obv. Face handsome and expressive. Letters of the word LIBERTY large and regular and very close to hair and milling. The B has been re-cut over an H to correct a blunder of the die-sinker, which gives the word the appearance of LIHERTY. Distance from the tip of the nose to the highest point of the letter R is 6½. The date is 4¾ long and curved a little more than on No. 81, which in other respects it strongly resembles. The 1 and 6, though very close to hair and bust, do not touch.

Rev.—*Rev. K.*—The ONE stands high and the CENT low within the wreath. A portion of the upright stroke of the T of CENT is concealed by a leaf. The distance from the final S of STATES to the top of the first A of AMERICA is 8. The right branch of the wreath has 19 leaves and 5 berries (only 3 depicted in the illustration), the left branch has 16 leaves and 6 berries. R[1].

No. 86.—Obv. This obverse is very similar to No. 81. It can be distinguished by the position of the figure 1 in the date in reference to the lowest lock on the head of Liberty, the distance being 1.

Rev.—*Rev. L.*—The letters TAT OF STATES and AME of AMERICA are connected at their feet. The right branch of the wreath has 18 leaves and 4 berries, the left 19 leaves and 4 berries. The right branch terminates above in a single leaf, which almost touches the terminal leaf of the left branch. The lowest leaf of the right branch almost touches the extreme end of the left foot of the final A of AMERICA. A pair of leaves is very close to OF. A leaf extends the full height of T of CENT. The lowest leaf on the left branch points toward U of UNITED. No leaves actually touch the letters, which is usually the case. The right wreath stem extends almost to the final A of AMERICA. Distance between the wreath stems is 5¼. The fraction stands very close to the knot; the figures are small and the dividing line short. R[1]. On some specimens of this number the obverse die is found with a crack extending along the tops of the letters T and Y of LIBERTY. This broken die is decidedly rare.

No. 87.—Obv. Similar to No. 81. Differing points lie solely in the date. Length, 4½. The tops of the figures are in a straight line. The 6 inclines to the right and is very close to the 9.

Rev.—*Rev. M.*—The letters of the word CENT stand decidedly crooked. The distance between ONE and CENT is 1½. The right branch of the wreath has 17 leaves and 5 berries; the left branch 18 leaves and 3 berries. The right branch terminates above in a single leaf, which points obliquely toward the terminal leaf of the left branch. The second leaf above the base on the right wreath branch almost touches the letter C of AMERICA, while two leaves are immediately below the left foot of the letter M. On the left branch the lowest group of leaves is opposite the letter N of UNITED. The fraction stands ¾ below the knot. The dividing line is straight and measures 2⅓, which is the full width of the denominator. R[1]. On some specimens of this number the profile of the head of Liberty appears double from the top of the forehead to the chin, evidently caused by an attempt to sharpen the die after it had been worn by long use. Specimens having this defect are decidedly rare.

No. 88.—Obv. The peculiarities of this obverse lie in the date and the border milling. The date is curved and measures 4⅓ in length. The figure 1 touches the hair. The distance from the top of the figure 1 to the lowest point of the letter L of LIBERTY is 11. The figure 6 touches the bust. Distance from the top of the figure 6 to the lowest point of the letter Y of LIBERTY is 10¾. The border milling is broad and deep on both obverse and reverse of this number, which in this particular resembles the cents of 1797.

Rev.—*Rev. N.*—The distance from the top of the final S of STATES to the top of the first A of AMERICA is 7½. The wreath strongly resembles that of *Rev. K.* It has 19 leaves and 5 berries on the right branch and 16 leaves and 3 berries on the left branch. (*Rev. K* has 6 berries on the left branch). The lowest leaf of the right branch points to the letter C of AMERICA. The right stem points to the right foot of the final A. R[1].

No. 89.—Obv. This die is marked by sundry small inequalities about the size of a period (.). One may be seen just above the figure 6 of the date, two in front of the neck and one on the upper curve of the letter R of LIBERTY. The date is straight and measures 5 in length. The figures 9 and 6 stand very close and are connected by a small die-crack, giving the date the appearance of 179-6. The figure 6 inclines to the right.

Rev.—*Rev. O.*—The words ONE and CENT stand closer than is the case with the preceding reverses, the distances between them being ½. The word CENT is distant 1¼ from the bow. The right branch of the wreath has 18 leaves and 6 berries, the left branch 14 leaves and 7 berries. The right branch terminates at the top in 2 leaves. The lowest leaf on the right branch points to the centre of the final A of AMERICA. A leaf touches the right foot of the letter M. The upper portions of the wreath stems—*i. e.*, those above the knot—are very irregular. The leaves do not actually touch any of the letters. There is a wide dividing space between the right and left wreath branches, ribbon ends and stems. Distance between the ribbon ends is 4. The figures of the fraction are small; the dividing line measures 1½. There is a small die-crack visible at the base of the letter E of UNITED. R[1]. On some specimens of this variety a die-crack extends along the tops of the letters T and Y of LIBERTY, as is also the case on some specimens of No. 86. A crack also extends from the left side of the letter T to the forelock, thence by way of the mouth to the milled border. Still another crack begins at the lowest curl, and extends through all the figures of the date. Specimens showing these die-cracks are not rare.

No. 90.—Obv. Peculiarities lie in the date. The date is curved and measures 5 in length. The figures are evenly spaced, and all incline toward the right. The distance from the bridge of the nose to the foot of the letter T of LIBERTY is 4.

Rev.—*Rev. O.* R[1].

No. 91.—Obv.—The letters L and I of the word LIBERTY are below the line of their fellows. The tail of the letter R is a simple slanting stroke which has its beginning inside the curve above. The date is almost straight. The figures 9 and 6 are upright and rather close. The figure 1 is somewhat distant from the hair. The distance from the lowest curl to the knob of the figure 6 is 5½. There is a small point on top of the 6.

Rev.—*Rev. O.* R[1].

No. 92.—Obv.—The date is curved and measures 4½ in length. The figures 9 and 5 incline to the left. The distance from the lowest curl to the knob of the figure 6 is 4¼. The figure 7 is very peculiar, both strokes being thick in comparison with the other figures of the date. A die-crack begins at the milled border and extends through the letter T to the forelock.

Rev.—*Rev. O.* R[4].

This embraces all the varieties of the cents of 1796 as yet discovered. The mint reports place the number of cents struck during this year at 974,700.

1797.

There is but one type of the cents of 1797, the Draped Bust, the same as the second type of the cents of 1796. During the year fourteen obverse and fourteen reverse dies were employed. Some of the cents of this year are found with milled edges, others have the edges plain.

The rev of D's #93 and 94 of 1797 looks exactly the same as rev. I of Gil's 1796. The plate of rev I in Gil's book is none too good and the only coin of 1796 Gil I I have is badly worn. Please check this. My G-I never too good but you are right.

Correct! HPN May 12/31—

G.H.C. 6/34—Have I Unc

of date at base, 5; distance between 1 and the first 7, at base, 1. The figures of the date are evenly spaced, and almost touch the bust. No!

Rev.—*Rev. A.*

Edges.—Milled in rude nicks and plain. R[1]. Specimens of this number occur showing a die crack, beginning at the border below the bust, passing through the date and curl to the border again on the left of the bust, thence following the border along the top of the word

JAMES G. MACALLISTER
3400 N. FIFTH STREET
PHILADELPHIA, PA.

May 27, 1933.

Dear Mr. Clapp:-

Yours of the 24th at hand. Note what you say about the 1798. This cent is in a collection consigned for auction; we are selling the collection on June 10, but the Cents were genera so poor that I did not include them in the catalog, as the expense of describing them would be greater than the receipts. I have written the owner to this effect and suggested that I would buy the lot at more than they would be likely to net at auction as I would have to bunch them up so in a sale that they would not bring anything. This '98 was the only Cent in the lot of any interest. As soon as I hear from him, will send you the coin, that is, if I can buy the lot, and if not will try to get this particular piece anyhow.

As to the explanation of the shifting of the die-sinking, the only thought that occurs to me in explanation is that some dies were not properly hardened, and bulged slightly on one side, making a depression on the other, then for some reason, probably an uneven planchet, bulged on the other sid sending the depressed area across the die. This sinking of the reverse dies seems to be characteristic of several of 1797, 98 and 1800, after which they probably found some better method of hardening the dies.

Have not heard from Newcomb since he wrote me about his earthquake experience, and did not know he was in the east. Hope he was not too hard hit in the Detroit Banks.

Yours very truly,

Mac

THE ABOVE GOODS ARE CONSIGNED ON APPROVAL AND THE TITLE IN THE CONSIGNOR DOES NOT PASS UNTIL THEY ARE PAID FOR.

June 16-20

Dear Sir Knapp

Well — hardly well, I mean. Been home now for a few days and find [illegible] accumulations during my two months away. Enjoying [illegible] I must confess California [illegible] "H-" [illegible] contributor on the [illegible] great [illegible] his arrangement. I threatened to write you [illegible], weather too fine to stay indoors still. Just brought home [illegible], my [illegible]; have the result and will give answer your query about 17-/-D.C." Doughty evidently is [illegible] on this matter as that piece with [illegible] [illegible] must have been the make [illegible] threat to [illegible]. The other [illegible] the figure 9 is either incomplete or not struck up as the ball is detached 9.

This is a distinct variety from D107 or may be a different die for that piece having the corner of the 7 touching the bust.

I will answer your other letters as soon as I can — it won't be very long. Maybe tomorrow if I can be left undisturbed for a while. I will lay out all my 1117's as in our list and study over your arrangement. I may be able to help you but if I can't it will [illegible] anyway.

The loaned [illegible] are [illegible] carefully [illegible] going [illegible] that I believe [illegible] very [illegible]. If you don't have these [illegible] welcome to keep them, without any —

See [illegible] 1797-[illegible]
[illegible]
991.1108

HOWARD R. NEWCOMB
119 Burlingame Avenue
DETROIT

May 30 '27

Dear Mr Clapp—

It looks as if there is something to the swell in the die after all in your #38 - D135. I have only one example of this number which you have seen. The Mills piece is very plain. I wonder what Mr Hines has - why don't you ask him!

Unfortunately I do not have the Cleneay sale catalogue & can't help you on #1814. I too have your #35 27-O but it is only in ordinary condition. With the careful watching that you & I have given to the 98's and no new numbers coming to light I'll bet a fishhook that Cleneay #1814 is your 27-O.

There are eight in your list of sales that I do not have but I do have the F. D. Taylor sale of June 1908. It has six plates - 5 of which are cents. I'll send it down for you to see if you wish and with it the Colvin Randall

I have checked over carefully your memo on 1797 - D98-99 & 108. You'll remember you drew me a picture of the breaks starting to left of L on certain denticules. Well, I affirm obv of 108 is same as 98 & 99. It is, [illegible] While 99 was going [illegible] as break is intermediate [illegible]

I notice in one of your recent letters you have secured an 1803, N3, 3^b=Cd; that is an improvement over your old example. The piece I have of this variety is almost poor, and if you don't know what to do with your duplicate & you think it will improve mine I would like to have it. The other piece, the 1802 N5, 4^b=Be I now have a very fi... example.

I didn't send a bid for Elder's sale just closed. There is one piece tho I was interested in # 2956 - 1802

HOWARD R. NEWCOMB
119 Burlingame Avenue
DETROIT

as 2955. Will be glad to hear your report on your purchases in this sale.

Have enclosed a rubbing of 1818 A8. If you ever saw this variety you would instantly recognize it as one you didn't have by the obv. rim breaks.

Am thinking quite seriously of driving thru to Cal., that is my son & self, wife & daughter will go by train. If I do will start June 18th. I can get a Packard service man to go with us, too, as he is anxious to go out to the coast, but more later about this.

Yours Sincerely
Howard R Newcomb

left wreath branches, ribbon ends and stems. Distance between the ribbon ends is 4. The figures of the fraction are small; the dividing line measures 1½. There is a small die-crack visible at the base of the letter E of U

die-crack extends

as is also the case

from the left side

mouth to the mill

curl, and extends

showing these die

No. 90.—Obv.

and measures 5 in

incline toward the

to the foot of the

Rev.—*Rev. O.*

No. 91.—Obv.—

the line of their f

stroke which has

almost straight.

The figure 1 is so

the lowest curl to the knob of the figure 6 is 5½. There is a small

1797.

There is but one type of the cents of 1797, the Draped Bust, the same as the second ... During the year fourteen
... ed. Some of the cents of
... ers have the edges plain.
... the cent of 1797 can be
... tate all are decidedly so,

... he word LIBERTY at top,
... Y, 2½; from tip of nose to
... ate at base, 4½; distance
... e end of down stroke of
... ay between the bust and
... xtreme end of the hair

... ath terminates at top in
... er reverse of the cents of
... s at their extreme ends,
... l stand very close to the

... appearance. R[4]. Speci-
... with a crack extending
... curving upward to the
... , between the letters E
... , and terminating at the

... e word LIBERTY at the
... he lowest point of Y, 3;
... left foot of L, 9¾; length
... first 7, at base, 1. The
... st touch the bust. No!

... R[1]. Specimens of this
... at the border below the
bust, passing through the date and curl to the border again on the left of the bust, thence following the border along the top of the word

1797 B-L
B Short L B L
93, 95 93, 95 97-96 97
98-99 98-99 101 - 101
100 100 102 - 102
104 107 104 103 - 103
108 108 105 105
N1 N1 180
N7 N7 ~~107 107~~
~~108 108~~
N4 & N5 104 104
N2 N2
N9 100/N1 N N8 N/107 N8
N7 N/96
Lo #94, 98, 97, 100, 101, 102,
103 - 105 - 106 107 - 108 - 109, N2, N6, N8
... 93 & 97
(Check this)

N - Per. D St. Top N - Br D
93 - 94 - 95 - 101 96 -
101 - 102 - 103 - 104 ...
107 - 108 ...
Per, No D
... N ..., N4, N5, N ..., N ...

left wreath branches, ri
ribbon ends is 4. The
line measures 1½. The
the letter E of UNITED.
die-crack extends alo
as is a
fron
mou
curl,
show
Nc
and i
inclii
to the
Re
No.
the lii
stroke
almost
The fi
the lov
point c
Rev.
No.
figures
to the
both st
date.
the lett
Rev.
This
ered.
this ye

1797.

There is but one type of the cents of 1797, the Draped Bust, the same as the second type of the cents of 1796. During the year fourteen obverse and fourteen reverse dies were employed. Some of the cents of this year are found with milled edges, others have the edges plain. In ordinary condition none of the varieties of the cent of 1797 can be termed very rare, but in fine or uncirculated state all are decidedly so, and command high prices.

No. 93.—Obv. *Measurements:* Length of the word LIBERTY at top, $10\frac{1}{2}$; from the tip of nose to nearest point of Y, $2\frac{1}{2}$; from tip of nose to extreme point of left foot of L, $9\frac{1}{3}$; length of date at base, $4\frac{1}{2}$; distance from right point of stand of the figure 1 to the end of down stroke of the first 7, $\frac{1}{3}$. The terminal 7 stands midway between the bust and the border. A die crack beginning at the extreme end of the hair ribbon extends to the border.

Rev.—*Rev. A.*—The right branch of the wreath terminates at top in a single leaf—a peculiarity existing on no other reverse of the cents of this year. Distance between the wreath stems at their extreme ends, $5\frac{2}{3}$. The figures of the fraction are small, and stand very close to the dividing line.

Edge.—Rudely milled, presenting a nicked appearance. R[4]. Specimens of the obverse die of this number occur with a crack extending from the shoulder across the hair, in a line curving upward to the border. Another crack begins at the border, between the letters E and R of LIBERTY, extending through E, B and I, and terminating at the border above.

No. 94.—Obv. *Measurements:* Length of the word LIBERTY at the top, $10\frac{3}{4}$; distance from the tip of nose to the lowest point of Y, 3; distance from tip of nose to extreme point of left foot of L, $9\frac{3}{4}$; length of date at base, 5; distance between 1 and the first 7, at base, 1. The figures of the date are evenly spaced, and almost touch the bust.

Rev.—*Rev. A.*

Edges.—Milled in rude nicks and plain. R[1]. Specimens of this number occur showing a die crack, beginning at the border below the bust, passing through the date and curl to the border again on the left of the bust, thence following the border along the top of the word

LIBERTY, terminating at a point opposite the chin. Specimens showing these cracks are decidedly rare.

Nos. 93 and 94 are the only dies of the cents of this year used in connection with milled edged planchets. The edges of the succeeding numbers are all plain.

No. 95.—Obv. *Measurements:* Length of the word LIBERTY at top, 11; distance from the tip of nose to nearest point of Y, 2; from figure 1 to the first 7, at base, ¾. The figure 1 touches the hair and the final 7 the bust. The 9 and final 7 are connected by a dash. A flaw in the die shows itself to the right of the neck.

Rev—*Rev. B.*—The letters of the words ONE and CENT are rude and much out of line; the space between the words measures but ¾. The right branch of the wreath terminates at the top in two leaves. There are 19 leaves and 5 berries on the right branch, and 16 leaves and 5 ~~4~~ berries on the left. The wreath stems are short and thick. Distance from end of right stem to letter A of AMERICA, ½. The figures of the fraction are small and very close together; the last cipher of the denominator stands somewhat above the line of the first. R[1]. On some specimens of this reverse a die crack occurs beginning at the berry opposite the letter M of AMERICA, passing through the leaves and the letter E of AMERICA to the border beyond. Specimens showing this die crack are decidedly rare.

No 96.—Obv. *Measurements:* Length of the word LIBERTY at top, 11; distance from tip of nose to lowest point of Y, 2¾; length of date at base, 4. The figures of the date are evenly spaced. The greater part of the cross stroke of the 7 touches the bust.

Rev.—*Rev. C.*—There are five berries on each branch of the wreath. A leaf touches the letter C of CENT. The figures of the fraction are large and widely spaced. *Measurements:* From the extreme point of right wreath stem to the letter A of AMERICA, 1; distance between the pendant ribbons ends, 4¾; distance between the words ONE and CENT, 1½; distance from letter D of UNITED to first S of STATES, 2; length of the dividing line of fraction, 1¾. R[1].

No. 97.—Obv. Same as No. 96.

Rev.—*Rev. D.*—The wreath has no projecting stems. *Measurements:* Distance between the pendant ribbon ends, 4¼; distance from the letter D of UNITED to the final A of AMERICA, 10⅓; distance between the letter D of UNITED to the first S of STATES, 2¼; distance between the words ONE and CENT, 1½. R⁴.

No. 98. Rev. E.

No. 98.—Obv. *Measurements:* Length of the word LIBERTY at top, 10½; distance from tip of nose to nearest point of Y, 2⅓; length of date at base, 4⅓. A flaw in the die shows as a dash crossing the letter R obliquely. A die crack begins at the border behind the head, and extends downward to the distance of 3.

Rev.—*Rev. E.*—The wreath has no projecting stems. The right pendant ribbon end has a string hanging beside it, extending its full length. *Measurements:* Distance between the ribbon ends, 5; distance from the letter D of UNITED to the final A of AMERICA, 11; distance from the D of UNITED to first S of STATES, 1½; distance between the words ONE and CENT, 1. R¹. Specimens of this combination occur with a perpendicular die crack in the field to the right of the bust.

No. 99.—Obv. Same as No. 98.

Rev.—*Rev. F.*—Closely resembles *Rev. C: Measurements:* Distance from the letter D of UNITED to the first S of STATES, 2½; distance from extreme point of right wreath stem to the final A of AMERICA, 1¼; length of the dividing line of fraction, 1½. R¹.

No. 100.—Obv. *Measurements*: Length of the word LIBERTY at top, 10¾; distance from tip of nose to the nearest point of Y, 2¼; distance from tip of nose to extreme point of left foot of L, 9¼; length of date at base, 4¼. The right corner of the final 7 touches the bust. A dash extends from the letter L to the letter B.

Rev.—*Rev. G.*—There are 6 berries on each branch of the wreath. There is no leaf touching the C of CENT. There are small open spaces on each side of the knot, caused by the ribbons being above the point where the stems cross. The figure 1 of the denominator is near the left ribbon. *Measurements*: Distance from the end of right wreath stem to the final A of AMERICA, ½; distance between the pendant ribbon ends, 4; distance from end of left wreath stem to U of UNITED, ½. A slight die crack crosses the two leaves, pointing toward the letter I of AMERICA. There is also a flaw, showing itself above the letter C. R^1.

No. 101.—Obv. *Measurements*: From the tip of nose to the nearest point of the letter Y, 3; length of date, 4¾; distance from the lowest curl to the figure 9 is 3. The letter T is immediately above the forelock. The final 7 of the date stands considerably below the bust, touching the border, and very close to the 9. A slight die crack appears on the left of the letter Y, just above its foot.

Rev.—*Rev. H.*—There are 5 berries on the right branch of the wreath, and 6 on the left. The right branch is thick, the left thin and delicate. The spaces on either side of the knot are larger than on *Rev. G.* The right pendant ribbon end touches the final A of AMERICA. The top of the right branch of the wreath terminates at the left of the final S of STATES. The numerator of the fraction is distant but ⅓ below the knot. R^1.

No. 102.—Obv. Same as No. 101.

Rev.—*Rev. I.*—There are 4 berries on the right, and 5 on the left branch of the wreath. The left stem is disconnected from the wreath, and is visible only on the left of the ribbon. There is an open space to the right of the knot. The lowest leaf on the left branch terminates opposite the left foot of the letter N of UNITED. The distance from the end of the left wreath stem to the letter U of UNITED is 1. R^1.

No. 103.—Obv. *Measurements*: From the tip of nose to the nearest point of the letter Y of LIBERTY, 2⅓; from the tip of nose to the extreme left point of the lower cross-stroke of the letter L, 9¼; length of the word LIBERTY at top, 10½; length of date, 4½; distance from the lowest curl to the figure 9, 2½. The letters of the word LIBERTY are slightly irregular, the B having too great an inclination to the right. The tail of the letter R is just above the forelock. The figure 1 just touches the hair and 7 the bust. The figure 9 stands midway between the first and last 7.

Rev.—*Rev. J.*—This reverse is readily distinguished from the fact that upon all circulated specimens, the word OF in the legend is obliterated. From some cause the surface of the die between the final S of STATES and the first A of AMERICA was sunk too deeply, producing a corresponding protuberance upon the coin, more susceptible to wear, of course, than other portions of the surface. There are 5 berries on either branch of the wreath; the left wreath stem points toward the letter N of UNITED; the lowest leaf on the left stem terminates opposite the right foot of the letter N of UNITED. A die crack connects the upper leaves of the pairs above the word ONE. *Measurements*: Length of wreath stems from point of union to terminus, right stem: 2¾; left stem: 2½; distance between the letter U of UNITED and the end of the left ribbon, ½; distance between the words ONE and CENT, 1¼; distance from the letter D of UNITED to the first S of STATES, 2; distance from the final S of STATES to the O in OF, 2. R[1].

No. 104.—Obv. *Measurements*: Length of the word LIBERTY at top, 10¼; distance from the tip of nose to the lowest point of the letter Y, 2¾. The letters B and T of LIBERTY are imperfect. The first 7 of the date is on a line with the 1. In other particulars, this obverse resembles No. 100.

Rev.—*Rev. K.*—The letters of the legend are all imperfectly formed and very irregular. A die crack connects the A and E of AMERICA, and the N and T of CENT at the top. There are 5 berries on either branch of the wreath; the branches are disconnected at base, on the left of the knot, the left stem terminating in a fine point near the letter U of UNITED. The dividing line of the fraction is curved and is connected by a slight line with the right ribbon end; the denominator of the fraction is curved. *Measurements*: Length of wreath stems from point of union to terminus, right stem: 2¼; left stem: 4½; space between the ribbon ends, 4⅗; length of the denominator of the fraction, 3; length of dividing line, 1⅓. R[4]. On some specimens of this variety a die crack appears upon the obverse, extending from the milled border directly behind the head downward to the lowest curl.

No. 105.—Obv. *Measurements*: Length of the word LIBERTY at the top, 10½; distance from the tip of nose to the nearest point of the letter Y, 2; distance from the tip of the nose to the extreme left point of the lower cross-stroke of the letter L, 9; length of date at base, 4¼.

Rev.—*Rev. K.* R[1].

No. 106.—Obv. *Measurements*: Length of the word LIBERTY, at top, 10½; distance from the tip of nose to the nearest point of the letter Y,

2$\frac{1}{3}$; distance from the tip of nose to the extreme left point of the lower cross-stroke of the letter L, 9$\frac{1}{4}$; length of date at base, 4; length of date at top, 3$\frac{3}{4}$. The tail of the R is just above the forelock. The figures of the date are closer together than on any other variety of this year; the 7 is very close to the bust, but does not touch it.

No. 106. Rev. L.

Rev.—*Rev. L.*—There are 6 berries on the right branch of the wreath and 5 on the left. The right wreath stem points to the right foot of the letter A of AMERICA. The extreme point of the right branch of the wreath at the top is parallel with the left perpendicular line of the final S of STATES. *Measurements*: Length of the word AMERICA, taken at base in a straight line from the extreme points of the first and last letters, 10; length of wreath stems from point of union to terminus, right stem: 2$\frac{2}{3}$; left stem: 2$\frac{1}{3}$; distance between the ribbon ends, 4$\frac{1}{3}$; distance from the D of UNITED to the first S of STATES; from the final S of STATES to the O in OF; from the F in OF to the first A in AMERICA, 1$\frac{1}{2}$ in each instance. The omission of the dividing line of the fraction in our illustration is a blunder. R[1].

No. 107.—Obv. *Measurements*: Length of the word LIBERTY at top, 10$\frac{2}{3}$; distance from the tip of nose to the nearest point of the letter Y, 2$\frac{1}{2}$; distance from the tip of nose to the extreme left point of the lower cross-stroke of the letter L, 9$\frac{1}{2}$; length of date at base, 4$\frac{1}{3}$; distance from the lowest curl to the first 7, 1$\frac{2}{3}$. The right corner of the final 7 touches the bust; the first 7 projects above the 1.

Rev.—*Rev. M.*—*Measurements*: Length of the word AMERICA, taken at base in a straight line from the extreme points of the first and last letters, 9$\frac{2}{3}$; length of wreath stems from point of union to terminus, right stem: 2$\frac{1}{2}$; left stem: 2$\frac{2}{3}$; distance between the ribbon ends, 4$\frac{1}{2}$; distance between the letter D of UNITED and the first

S of STATES, 1⅔; distance between the letter F in OF to the first A of AMERICA at base, 2; length of denominator, 3¼; distance from the top of the figure 1 of the denominator to the end of the right wreath stem, 4⅓. R[1]. On some specimens of this variety, a die crack is found beginning at a point on the milled border behind the head, distant 4½ from the letter L, thence extending downward toward the shoulder.

No. 108.—Obv. This variety may be distinguished by an extra outline behind the head, extending downward along the hair to the first curl below the knot. The upper half of the letter B is imperfect, and the crosslet of the letter E is united with the upper cross-stroke. *Measurements*: Distance from the tip of the nose to the nearest point of the letter Y, 2½; distance from the tip of the nose to the lower left point of the letter L, 9½; length of date at base, 4⅓; distance from the first 7 to the nearest curl, 1.

Rev.—*Rev. N.*—This reverse can be distinguished at a glance. The letter M of AMERICA is cut over an E, the outlines of the latter still being quite distinct. The crosslets of all letters E on this reverse unite with the upper cross-stroke. The loops of the bow are disconnected from the wreath. R[1].

No. 109.—Obv. The letters of the word LIBERTY are widely spaced; the R touches the hair. The figures of the date are nearer the bust than on other varieties, and the right and left corners of the final 7 touch. The top of the figure 1 touches the hair. *Measurements*: Length of the word LIBERTY at the top, 11; length of date, 4½.

Rev.—*Rev. N.* R[1]. On some specimens of this variety, a die crack shows itself on the obverse, beginning at the right of the bust near the drapery, and extending in a curved line to the border milling. Another begins at the bust near the neck, and extends downward to the border milling. A third begins at a point above the first 7 of the date, and extends through the hair to the border milling on the left.

No. 109 closes the list of the cents of 1797. The mint records show that the number issued during the year was 897,510.

1798.

The cents of 1798 are of the same general design as those of the preceding year. The varieties of die, of which there are many, will be found in all cases to be very slight and can only be detected by careful comparison with the measurements below. The cents of 1798 were struck upon planchets with edges both plain and milled. It is useless to attempt to make varieties of the edgés, as specimens from any one of the differing combinations of dies are liable to turn up at any time struck upon planchets the edges of which are either plain or milled; but where certain combinations are usually found struck upon milled edged planchets, the fact will be mentioned. The cents of 1798 are the commonest of any struck during the last century. Certain combinations, however, are somewhat difficult to procure and these will be found indicated at the end of the description in the usual way. It is a comparatively easy matter to obtain fine specimens of the common varieties of the cents of this year at a moderate price.

No. 110.—Obv. *Measurements:* Length of word LIBERTY at top, 11¼; distance from the tip of the nose to the nearest point of the letter Y, 2; length of date at base, 5⅜. The figures of the date evenly spaced and stand on a curve. The 1 is very close to the lowest curl; the 7 is short and thick; the 8 is small and touches the bust. A slight die crack beginning at the hair passes downward, touching the top and bottom of the figure 7. Another crack connects the 7 and 9 at top. The border milling is wide and the planchet large. This variety is usually termed the *Spread Date.*

Rev.—*Rev. A.*—This is the same die as No. 76, *Rev. E*, of the cents of 1796. The letters A and M of AMERICA are connected at the feet. The lowest leaf on the left branch of the wreath points toward the space between the letters U and N of UNITED. The lowest leaf of a group of three on the right branch touches the right foot of the letter A of AMERICA; the lowest leaf of a similar group on the left branch touches the N of UNITED. The branches terminate in single leaves at top. Length of both wreath stems from point of union to terminus, 3. The figures of the denominator of the fraction are small and close. R^4.

No. 111.—Obv. This die is the same as No. 96. The terminal 7 of the date having been altered to an 8 that it might do duty another year. *Measurements:* Length of word LIBERTY at top, 11; distance from the tip of the nose to the nearest point of the letter Y, 2¾; distance from tip of nose to the lower left point of the letter L, 9⅔; length of date at base, 4½. The figure 8 is broader than the 7. The tips of the 7 over which the 8 has been placed rise slightly above the latter figure and touch the bust. The border milling is wide.

Rev.—*Rev. B.*—The right branch of the wreath has 19, and the left, 16 leaves; there are 5 berries on either branch. The right branch terminates at top in two leaves [with these particulars all varieties following agree]; the wreath stems are short and narrower near the ribbons than at the ends. The group of two leaves on the left branch opposite the letters ED of UNITED stands almost perpendicular. The lowest leaf on the left branch terminates midway between the feet of the letter N of UNITED. *Measurements:* Length of both wreath stems from point of union to terminus, 2⅓; length of denominator of the fraction, 2¾. R^4.

No. 112.

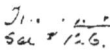

No. 112.—Obv. This obverse is likewise altered from one of the dies of the preceding year. The letters E and R of the word LIBERTY touch the hair. The upright stroke of the figure 7 is short and clumsy; the 8 touches the bust. In other particulars it is the same as No. 111.

Rev.—*Rev. C.*—The wreath stems are short and thick, the right stem being slightly curved. A die crack beginning at the lower leaf of of the left branch of the wreath, passes through the numerator of the fraction and thence to a point on the border opposite the final A of AMERICA. Another crack beginning at the A of STATES, terminates at the first A of AMERICA R^4.

No. 113.—Obv. This obverse is likewise altered from one of the dies of the preceding year. *Measurements:* Length of word LIBERTY at top, 10⅔; distance from the tip of the nose to the nearest point of the letter Y, 2½; distance from tip of nose to the lower left point of the letter L, 9½; distance from the tip of the nose to the lower right point of the letter E, 6; length of date at base, 4⅔; distance from the figure 1 to the lowest curl, ½. The letters E and R are very close to the hair, but do not touch. The figure 8 does not touch the bust. All the figures of the date are very close to the border milling, but none touch. The border milling is narrow.

Rev.—*Rev. D.*—The left branch of the wreath opposite the letters E and D of UNITED is vine-like and wavy. The lowest leaf on the right branch terminates near the right foot of the letter N of UNITED. *Measurements*: Distance between the letter D of UNITED and the first S of STATES, 2; distance between the F in OF and the first A of AMERICA, 2⅓; length of wreath stems from point of union to terminus, right stem: 2½, left stem: 3; length of denominator of fraction, 3¼. R[1].

No. 114.—Obv. *Measurements*: Length of word LIBERTY at top, 10⅓; distance from the tip of the nose to the nearest point of the letter Y, 2¼; distance from tip of nose to the lower left point of the letter L, 9¼; length of date at base, 4¾. The figures of the date are evenly spaced. The 1 is a little nearer the curl than on No. 113. The 8 is large and stands midway between bust and the border milling, which is wide.

Rev.—*Rev. B.* R[1].

No. 115.—Obv. *Measurements*: Length of date at base, 4½; distance between the figure 1 and the lowest curl, ⅔. In other particulars the measurements agree with No. 114. The foot of the letter R just touches the hair. The figures of the date are well formed and stand close together. The 8 is large and stands midway between the bust and the border milling, which is wide.

Rev.—*Rev. E.*—The branches of the wreath are thin, but well proportioned; the lowest leaf on the inside of the left branch is indistinct, being a mere outline which extends to the back of the letter C of CENT. The wreath stems are short. The dividing line of the fraction tapers to a point, touching the ribbon on the right and being quite distant from the figure 1 of the denominator. Immediately below the knot is a small point about the size of a period. *Measurements*: Distance from the tip of the lowest leaf on the left branch of the wreath to the left foot of the letter N of UNITED, ⅗; distance from the tip to the highest leaf on the right branch of the wreath to the top of the letter O in OF, 3⅓; length of both wreath stems from point of union to terminus, 2½; length of denominator of fraction, 2⅜. The edge of this variety is found milled with slanting strokes, very slightly impressed and seldom visible all around the planchet. It is also found struck upon planchets having a plain edge. R[4].

No. 116.—Obv. *Measurements:* Length of word LIBERTY at top, 10½; distance from the tip of the nose to nearest point of the letter Y, 2⅓; distance from tip of nose to the lower left point of the letter L, 9⅓; length of date at base, 4¾; distance between the figures 7 and 9 at top, ½. The foot of the letter R touches the hair. The date is curved, evenly spaced and the figure 8 large. The border milling is narrow.

Rev.—*Rev. F.*—The branches of the wreath are thick and heavy; the tops of both terminate just below the letter E of STATES. The lowest leaf on the inside of the left branch is very close to the letter C of CENT but does not touch. The letter A of STATES is below the line of its fellows and the final S above. The letters A and M of AMERICA connect at the feet. The dividing line of the fraction is short and the final 0 of the denominator very close to the ribbon end. *Measurements:* Length of wreath stems from point of union to terminus, right stem: 2¾, left stem: 3; distance between the extreme points of the ribbon ends, 4; width of denominator of fraction, 2½. Edge milled. R[1].

No. 117.—Obv. *Measurements:* Length of word LIBERTY at top, 10¼; distance from the tip of the nose to the nearest point of the letter Y, 2½; distance from tip of nose to the lower left point of the letter L, 9⅓; length of date at base, 4⅔. The figure 7 of the date is above the line of the 1 and 8, and the figure 9 below. The 8 is large and upright, while the other figures slant to the right. The 9 has a small projecting point on the right side at top. The border milling is narrow.

Rev.—*Rev. G.*—The letters A and M of AMERICA connect at the feet. The figures of the denominator of the fraction are widely spaced. *Measurements:* Length of wreath stems from point of union to terminus, right stem: 2⅔, left stem: 2¾; distance between the extreme points of the ribbon ends, 4⅓; length of denominator of fraction, 3. R[1]. Some specimens of this variety occur showing a die crack on the obverse, beginning at the top of the letter E and extending along the tops of the letters RTY to the border milling. Specimens showing this crack are decidedly rare.

Rev G [illegible] I

No. 118.—Obv. *Measurements*: Length of word LIBERTY at the top, $10\frac{3}{4}$; distance from the tip of the nose to the nearest point of the letter Y, 3; distance from the tip of the nose to the lower left point of the letter, L, $9\frac{3}{4}$; space between the letter R and the hair, $\frac{1}{3}$; length of date at base, 5. The date is curved and evenly spaced, the 8 is large, the 7 small. There is a small protuberance, the result of a nick on the die, just below the chin. The border milling is narrow.

Rev.—*Rev. II.*—A leaf on the inside of the left branch of the wreath just touches the letter C of CENT. A leaf on the inside of the right branch ends a little above the base of the letter T of CENT. A small scratch in the die—hardly a crack—shows itself at the letter E of UNITED and again at the right foot of the letter M of AMERICA. On some specimens this scratch appears as a faint line between those points. *Measurements*: Distance between the highest leaf on the right branch of the wreath to the top of the letter A of STATES, $4\frac{3}{4}$; distance from the same leaf to the top of O in OF, $3\frac{3}{4}$; length of wreath stems from point of union to terminus, right stem: $2\frac{3}{4}$; left stem: $2\frac{1}{2}$; distance between the pendant ribbon ends, $4\frac{1}{4}$; length of denominator, $2\frac{2}{3}$; length of the dividing line of the fraction, $1\frac{1}{3}$. R[1]. Examples from both dies of this number are found in a badly cracked condition. Of the obverse die specimens occur with a crack beginning at the border below the letter Y, and extending through the eye to the hair ribbon. Another begins at the letter B, and extending downward joins the transverse crack; another still passes through the bust. A crack on the reverse die begins at the first T of STATES, and extends to the N of CENT. Another begins at the top of the O in OF, and extends downward to a group of three leaves on the right branch of the wreath. On these cracked specimens the scratch extending from the E of STATES to the M of AMERICA, spoken of above, is more prominent, and another shows itself between the dividing line of the fraction and the right ribbon end which it crosses. On other specimens still, there is a crack which begins at the milled border, passes through the E of STATES thence curving downward through the wreath and the fraction to the border again. This variety seems to have been touched up with a graver, as the letters are thicker, and the C entirely out of shape.

No. 119.—Obv. *Measurements*: Length of word LIBERTY at the top, 11;

distance from the tip of the nose to the nearest point of the letter Y, 3; distance from the tip of the nose to the lower left point of the letter L, 10; distance from the lowest curl to the figure 7, $1\frac{1}{3}$; length of date at base, 5. The figure 8 is small.

Rev.—*Rev. H.* R¹.

No. 120.—Obv. *Measurements*: Length of word LIBERTY at the top, $10\frac{1}{2}$; distance from the tip of the nose to the nearest point of the letter, Y, $2\frac{2}{3}$; distance from the tip of the nose to the lower left point of the letter L, $9\frac{3}{4}$; length of date at base, $5\frac{1}{3}$. The letter R is very close to the hair; the figure 8 is large, and the 1 just touches the lowest curl; the milled border is narrow. A slight crack in the die extends from the milled border on the left through the hair to the tops of the figures 1 and 7.

Rev.—*Rev. I.*—The letters A and M of AMERICA are connected at the base. *Measurements*: From the tip of the highest leaf on the right branch of the wreath to the top of the letter O in OF, $3\frac{1}{4}$; length of wreath stems from point of union to terminus, right stem: $2\frac{1}{2}$; left stem: $2\frac{3}{4}$; distance between the pendant ribbon ends, $4\frac{1}{2}$; length of denominator of fraction, 3. This die shows a short crack extending from the milled border to the top of the last T of STATES R¹. On some specimens of this number a break in the die in front of the bust occurs, measuring $4\frac{1}{2}$ in length.

No. 121.—Obv. *Measurements*: Length of word LIBERTY at the top, $11\frac{1}{4}$; distance from the tip of the nose to the nearest point of the letter Y, $3\frac{1}{4}$; distance from the tip of the nose to the lower left point of the letter L, 10; length of date at base, $4\frac{3}{4}$. The figure 8 is small. The border milling is narrow. This die was badly broken and for that reason can be readily identified. On the right, at the milled border opposite the face, the most prominent break shows itself; a crack passes through the letter T, touching the base of the Y, crosses the break and extends downward to the border near the bust. Another imperfection in the die shows itself as a small lump about the size of a period opposite the eye.

Rev.—*Rev. H.* R¹. When found combined with this obverse, *Rev. H* presents a slight crack beginning at a point below the final 0 of the fraction, passing upward through the bases of the letters A and C of AMERICA to the top of the letter I, and terminating at the milled border beyond. This crack may be the result of using the die in combination with the cracked obverse, as its position is directly opposite the obverse crack, while it is also of the same length. On the other hand specimens are found which would seem to cast a doubt upon this theory, showing the obverse crack passing through the letter T and the base of the Y to a point on the milled border opposite the nose, while the reverse die-crack below the fraction curves upward through the letters E and M of AMERICA to the border, and another slight crack extends from the first 0 of the fraction to the lowest leaf on the left branch of the wreath, and this in addition to the scratch mentioned in the full description of this reverse, as extending from the letter E of UNITED to the letter M of AMERICA.

No. 122.—Obv. *Measurements*: Length of word LIBERTY at the top, $10\frac{1}{2}$; distance from the tip of the nose to the nearest point of the letter Y, 3; distance from the tip of the nose to the lower left point of of the letter L, $9\frac{3}{4}$; length of date at base, $4\frac{1}{2}$. The figure 8 is small. A small dash touches the tail of the letter R. The border milling is narrow. An irregular scratch in the die shows itself upon the neck, crossing the field to the border milling beyond.

Rev.—*Rev. J.*—The letters A M and E of AMERICA are connected at base; the letter C of AMERICA is imperfect, a small bar of copper running through its centre; the lower portion of the wreath, particularly on the left branch, is also imperfect; the lowest leaf on the left branch terminates opposite the left foot of the letter N of UNITED. The figure 1 of the denominator is quite distant from the two ciphers. *Measurements*: From the highest leaf on the right branch of the wreath to the top of the letter O in OF, $3\frac{3}{4}$; from the same leaf to the top of the letter A of STATES, $4\frac{3}{8}$; distance from the letter D of UNITED to the first S of STATES, $1\frac{1}{4}$. Length of wreath stems from point of union to terminus, right stem: $2\frac{1}{2}$, left stem: $2\frac{3}{4}$; distance between the pendant ribbon ends, 5; length of denominator of the fraction, $2\frac{3}{8}$. R^{3}.

No. 123.—Obv. Same as No. 122, but struck before the die became scratched.

Rev.—*Rev. K.*—The lowest leaf on the left branch of the wreath terminates opposite the right foot of the letter N of UNITED. The figures of the fraction are well spaced. *Measurements*: Length of word AMERICA at top, $10\frac{1}{3}$; distance from the letter D of UNITED to the first S of STATES, 2; length of wreath stems from the point of union to terminus, right stem: $2\frac{2}{3}$; left stem: $2\frac{1}{3}$; distance between the pendant ribbon ends, $4\frac{1}{3}$; length of the dividing line of the fraction, $1\frac{1}{2}$. R[1].

No. 124.—Obv. *Measurements*: Length of word LIBERTY at top, 11; length of date at base, $4\frac{3}{4}$. The figure 8 is small, and the 9 stands lower than its fellows. The border milling is narrow.

Rev.—*Rev. L.*—*Measurements*: From the highest leaf on the right branch of the wreath to the top of the letter O in OF, $3\frac{1}{2}$; from the same leaf to the top of the letter A of STATES, 5; distance from the letter D of UNITED to the first S of STATES, $2\frac{1}{4}$; length of wreath stems from point of union to terminus, right stem: $2\frac{1}{8}$; left stem: $2\frac{2}{3}$; distance between the pendant ribbon ends, $4\frac{1}{4}$; length of denominator of the fraction, 3. A die-crack beginning at the final A of AMERICA extends to the ribbon. R[1].

No. 125.—Obv. Same as No. 124.

Rev.—*Rev. H.* R[1]. In this combination the obverse die is sometimes found cracked from the centre of the forehead through the letter Y to the border, and again from the throat downward across the field to the milled border near the bust.

No. 126.—Obv. *Measurements*: Length of word LIBERTY at the top, $10\frac{1}{2}$; distance from the tip of the nose to the nearest point of the letter Y, $3\frac{1}{4}$; distance from the tip of the nose to the lower left point of the letter L, $9\frac{3}{4}$; length of date at base, $4\frac{2}{3}$. The figure 8 is small.

Rev.—*Rev. M.*—This reverse may be readily distinguished by the position of the lower leaf on the inside of the left branch of the wreath, which is quite distant from the letter C of CENT, occurring on no other reverse of the cents of this year. The letters are all very widely spaced. *Measurements*: Distance from the highest leaf on the right branch of the wreath to the letter O in OF, $2\frac{1}{2}$; distance from the same leaf to the top of the letter A of STATES, $5\frac{3}{4}$; distance from the letter D of UNITED to the first S of STATES, $1\frac{1}{4}$; distance from the final S of STATES to the O in OF, 1; length of wreath stems from point of union to terminus, right stem: $2\frac{3}{4}$; left stem: $2\frac{1}{2}$. A die-crack beginning at the letter T of STATES passes through the E, downward through the leaves of the left branch to the letters I T and E of UNITED and thence to the milled border beyond. R[1].

No. 127.—Obv. Same as No. 126, but the die now appears cracked across the field behind the head in three lines.

Rev.—*Rev. N.*—The figure 1 of the denominator is quite distant from the ciphers, the dividing line terminates in a point very close to the right ribbon end. *Measurements*: Distance from the highest leaf on right branch of the wreath to the letter O in OF, 3; distance from the same leaf to the top of the letter A of STATES, 4¾; length of the word AMERICA at base, 9½; distance from the letter D of UNITED to the first S of STATES, 1½; distance from the final S of STATES to the O in OF, 1½; length of wreath stems from point of union to terminus, right stem: 3¼; left stem: 3¼; distance between the pendant ribbon ends, 4½; length of denominator of the fraction, 3; length of the dividing line, 2½. The final S of STATES shows a slight die-crack on the left, extending upward to the milled border. R[1].

No. 128.—Obv. *Measurements:* Length of word LIBERTY at the top, 11⅛; distance from the tip of the nose to the nearest point of the letter Y, 3; distance from the tip of the nose to the lower left point of the letter L, 10; space between the letter R and the hair, ⅛; length of date at base, 5; distance from lowest curl to the figure 7, 1½. The figure 8 is small. A slight scratch in the die appears on the left of the letter T, while a crescent-shaped crack is seen in the field, behind the head, passing through the hair ribbon and measuring 9 in length.

Rev.—*Rev. H.*—When found in this combination, *Rev. H* does not show the die-crack alluded to in its description. R[1].

No. 129.—Obv. *Measurements:* With the exception of the length of date at base, which is 4¾, the measurements of this obverse correspond with those of No. 128. The figure 8 is small.

Rev.—*Rev. H.*—Does not show the die-crack. R[1].

No. 130.—Obv. *Measurements:* Distance from the tip of the nose to the nearest point of the letter Y, 2¼; distance from the tip of the nose to the lower left point of the letter L, 9¾; length of date at base, 5¼; distance from lowest curl to the figure 9, 2¾. The forelock is between the letters R and T; the R is near the hair; the figure 7 has a decided slant to the right; the 8 is small.

Rev.—*Rev. H.*—In combination with this obverse, Rev. H sometimes shows a die-crack connecting the tops of the letters ATES with the border milling. R^{1}. R. H.

No. 131.—Obv. *Measurements:* Length of word LIBERTY at the top, 10$\frac{3}{8}$; distance from the tip of the nose to the nearest point of the letter Y, 2$\frac{3}{4}$; distance from the tip of the nose to the lower left point of the letter L, 9$\frac{3}{8}$; length of date at base, 4$\frac{3}{4}$. The letters T and Y are larger than their fellows. The figure 8 is small.

Rev.—*Rev. N.*—When found in combination with this obverse, Rev. N shows the die-crack from the border to final S of STATES extended to the base of the adjoining letter E, and thence through T, touching the border again above A. R^{1}.

No. 132.—Obv. *Measurements:* Length of word LIBERTY at the top, 11$\frac{1}{4}$; distance from the tip of the nose to the nearest point of the letter Y, 3$\frac{1}{2}$; distance from the tip of the nose to the lower left point of the letter L, 10; length of date at base, 4$\frac{3}{8}$; distance from the lowest curl to the figure 9, 2$\frac{3}{8}$. There is a die-crack connecting the tops of the letters RTY. The figure 8 is small. Dat. straight.

Rev.—*Rev. H.*—Shows the die-crack noticed in No. 128. R^{1}.

No. 133.—Obv. *Measurements:* Length of word LIBERTY at the top, 11; distance from the tip of of the nose to the nearest point of the letter Y, 3$\frac{1}{8}$; distance from the tip of the nose to the lower left point of the letter L, 9$\frac{3}{4}$; length of date at base, 4$\frac{3}{4}$; distance from the lowest curl to the figure 9, 2$\frac{3}{4}$. The figure 8 is small. There is a die-crack at the border near the letter L, measuring 4$\frac{1}{2}$ in length and 1$\frac{1}{3}$ in width.

Rev.—*Rev. H.*—Shows the die-crack noticed in No. 128. R^{1}.

No. 134.—Obv. *Measurements:* Length of word LIBERTY at the top, 11; distance from the tip of the nose to the nearest point of the letter Y, 3$\frac{1}{4}$; distance from the tip of the nose to the lower left point of the letter L, 10; length of date at base, 5; distance from the lowest curl to the figure 9, 2$\frac{3}{4}$. The figure 8 is small.

Rev.—*Rev. G.*—When found combined with this obverse, Rev. G presents a singular die-crack beginning at the denominator of the fraction, and connecting all the letters of the legend at their tops, nearly completing the circuit of the planchet. R[1].

No. 135.

Rev. O.

No. 135.—Obv. *Measurements* : Length of word LIBERTY at the top, 11⅛ ; distance from the tip of the nose to the nearest point of the letter Y, 3¼ ; distance from the tip of the nose to the lower left point of the letter L, 10 ; length of date at base, 4⅔. The top of the figures of the date are in a straight line. The 8 is small.

Rev.—*Rev. O.—Measurements* : Distance from the tip of the highest leaf on the right branch of the wreath to the top of the letter O in OF, 4 ; distance from the same point to the top of the letter A of STATES, 4¾ ; length of wreath stems from point of union to terminus, right stem : 2⅔ ; left stem : 2⅔ ; distance between the ribbon ends, 4⅛ ; length of denominator of the fraction, 2⅔. The crosslet of the letter E of AMERICA is connected with the upper and lower horizontal strokes (not so represented in our illustration); on the lower part of the same letter, at the left, is a small point. R[1].

No. 136.—Obv. *Measurements* : Length of the word LIBERTY at top, 11¼ ; distance from the tip of the nose to the nearest point of the letter Y, 3⅛ ; distance from the tip of the nose to the lower left point point of the letter L, 10 ; length of date at base, 4¾ ; distance from the lowest curl to the figure 9, 2½. The figure 8 is small. This die appears to have been pretty badly broken up. One crack, beginning at the border milling on the right of the figure 8, extends upward to the bust, thence passing to the left through the hair to the border beyond. Another, beginning at the border at a point 4 above the one just mentioned, also extends across the hair. Another, beginning at the forelock, extends through the base of the letter Y. Another, very close and parallel with the last, extends to the letter T. Another still, connects all the letters of the word LIBERTY at the top.

Rev.—*Rev. P.*—This reverse differs from all others of the cents of this year in several particulars which aid in its ready detection. The left branch of the wreath bears *six* berries instead of five, as appear upon all other reverses of the year; the berries are all very small. The letter N in each of the three instances of its employment is larger than its fellows. The figures of the fraction, also are much larger than usual, the 00 showing the outline of smaller ciphers inside. The dividing line of the fraction terminates near the ribbons on both sides with ends cut squarely off. *Measurements*: Distance from the tip of the highest leaf on the right branch of the wreath to the top of the letter O in OF, $3\frac{3}{8}$; distance from the same point to the top of the letter A of STATES, $4\frac{3}{4}$; distance between ONE and CENT, $\frac{3}{8}$; distance from the letter D of UNITED to the first S of STATES, $2\frac{1}{8}$; distance from the F in OF to the first A of AMERICA, $2\frac{1}{8}$; length of denominator of the fraction, $2\frac{3}{4}$; length of the dividing line of fraction, $1\frac{3}{8}$; distance between the top of the numerator and the knot, $\frac{1}{8}$; length of wreath stems from point of union to terminus, right stem: $2\frac{1}{2}$; left stem: $2\frac{1}{2}$; distance between the ribbon ends, $3\frac{3}{4}$. R[4].

No. 136 terminates the list of the cents of 1798. The number issued, according to the records of the mint, was 979,700. Although the cents of 1798 are not rare with the exception of the few varieties noted, they are still sufficiently scarce to render it a work of perseverance to complete the series, but since dealers seldom trouble themselves to pick over their stocks of the cents of common dates for varieties, with patience all mentioned in this list can be obtained at a moderate price.

1799.

The cents of the year 1799 are the rarest of the copper issues of the United States mint. There exist but two varieties of obverse and two of reverse of the cents of this year, so far as we have been able to ascertain.

This statement, published in the JOURNAL in July, 1880, Vol. V, has been contradicted but not successfully refuted. Dr. Dickeson, in his

American Numismatic Manual, 1860, claims for the cent of 1799, four varieties, but since he gives no hint as to the nature of these variations, his statement is entitled to no weight. Another and later compiler of information relating to the cents of the United States, makes three varieties of obverse; his third variety is not satisfactory, however, for it is evidently from the same die as one of the others described, the variations claimed being but the result of wear.

At the time our former list made its appearance, its compiler probably enjoyed better opportunity for comparison of specimens of the cents of 1799 than will ever be afforded to any future writer upon this theme.

Then the JOURNAL could offer but two varieties of obverse and two of reverse; nor has eight years of close observation of the specimens of the cent of 1799 which have passed through the hands of our publishers, the Scott Stamp and Coin Co., L'd., as well as the most careful scrutiny of those specimens exhibited on the auction boards, revealed any variations of die, beyond those which we are about to describe.

The cents of 1799 are never found in an uncirculated condition; indeed the large majority of the specimens found in the cabinets of collectors are so much worn as to render their date and genuineness a matter of doubt.

Why the cents of 1799 should be so rare, when according to the mint records the issue was 904,585, is a question which has never been satisfactorily answered. The story of their shipment in large quantities to the coast of Africa by a firm in Salem, Mass., formerly accepted by collectors, is not now credited. Rare they are and rare they always will be, but the reason must remain one of the mysteries to the end of time.

No. 137.—Obv. *Measurements*: Length of word LIBERTY at base, $9\frac{1}{8}$; distance from the tip of the nose to the nearest point of the letter Y, $3\frac{1}{2}$; distance from the tip of the nose to the lower left point of the letter L, 10; length of date through the centre, $4\frac{1}{2}$; distance from the figure 1 to the lowest curl, $\frac{1}{2}$; distance from the figure 7 to the lowest curl, $1\frac{1}{8}$. The letter E is a little below the line of its fellows. The date is evenly spaced; the final 9 stands perfectly upright and exhibits beneath it traces of an 8, showing that this variety was struck from an altered die of the preceding year, indicated particularly by a line which connects the knob of the 9 with the loop forming the body of the figure.

No. 137. Rev. A

Rev.—*Rev. A.*—The letters of the legend are evenly spaced. A leaf touches the letter C of CENT, which is below the line of its fellows. The figures of the fraction are small and well shaped, *Measurements*: Length of word AMERICA at base, 9¾; length of wreath stems from point of union to terminus, right stem : 2¾; left stem : 2¼; distance between the ribbon ends, 4⅓; length of denominator, 2½; length of the dividing line of fraction, 1½. R⁵.

oase,
let-
nt of
from
7 to
paced;
al 9 in-
clines ... border.

American Numismatic Manual, 1860, claims for the cent of 1799, four varieties, but since he gives no hint as to the nature of these variations, his statement is entitled to no weight. Another and later compiler of information relating to the cents of the United States, makes three varieties of obverse; his third variety is not satisfactory, however, for it is evidently from the same die as one of the others described, the variations claimed being but the result of wear.

At the time our former list made its appearance, its compiler probably enjoyed better opportunity for comparison of specimens of the cents of 1799 than will ever be afforded to any future writer upon this theme.

Then the JOURNAL could offer but two varieties of obverse and two of reverse; nor has eight years of close observation of the specimens of the cent of 1799 which have passed through the hands of our publishers, the Scott Stamp and Coin Co., L'd., as well as the most careful scrutiny of those specimens exhibited on the auction boards, revealed any variations of die, beyond those which we are about to describe.

The cents of 1799 are never found in an uncirculated condition; indeed the large majority of the specimens found in the cabinets of collectors
a matter of
Why the
mint record
been satisf
quantities
accepted by
they alway
to the end
No. 137.
9⅓; distan
Y, 3½; dista
ter L, 10; le
1 to the lo
1½. The l

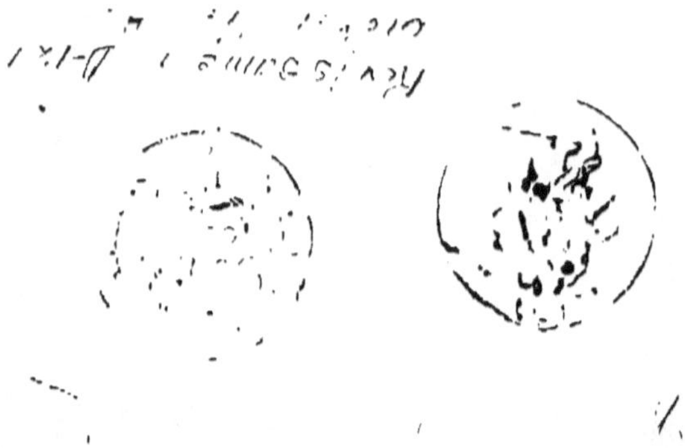

evenly spaced; the final 9 stands perfectly upright and exhibits beneath it traces of an 8, showing that this variety was struck from an altered die of the preceding year, indicated particularly by a line which connects the knob of the 9 with the loop forming the body of the figure.

No. 137. Rev. A

Rev.—*Rev. A.*—The letters of the legend are evenly spaced. A leaf touches the letter C of CENT, which is below the line of its fellows. The figures of the fraction are small and well shaped, *Measurements*: Length of word AMERICA at base, 9¾; length of wreath stems from point of union to terminus, right stem: 2¾; left stem: 2¼; distance between the ribbon ends, 4⅓; length of denominator, 2½; length of the dividing line of fraction, 1½. R[3].

No. 138. Rev. B.

No. 138.—Obv. *Measurements*: Length of word LIBERTY at base, 9½; distance from the tip of the nose to the nearest point of the letter Y, 3½; distance from the tip of the nose to the lower left point of the letter, L, 10¼; length of date through the centre, 4⅛; distance from the figure 1 to the lowest curl, ¾; distance from the figure 7 to the lowest curl, 1½. The date is curved and not evenly spaced; the knobs of the 99 are thick and turn up sharply; the final 9 inclines toward its fellow. Only traces of milling appear at the border.

Rev.—*Rev. B.*—This reverse is believed to be from the same die as reverse A after it had been worked over with the graver. The letters and figures appear larger from this cause. *Rev. B* presents a peculiarity which will enable the collector to readily distinguish it from *Rev. A.* This is a small projection between the letter T of CENT and the letter E of ONE. It is believed to be due to the removal of a small scale of steel from the die at the time of retouching. It invariably appears on *Rev. B* and is never found on *Rev. A.* R⁷.

Any cent bearing the date 1799, not exhibiting the peculiarities and corresponding with the measurements given above, may be safely set down as a counterfeit. Certainly it should not be accepted without subjecting it to the rigid scrutiny of some recognized authority in this particular department of numismatic science.

The spurious cents of this date most commonly offered are alterations from 1798. A good glass will generally reveal the truth in this particular, although we have seen instances where the alteration had been so skillfully performed as to render the closest observation necessary for its detection.

1800.

The varieties of the cent of the year 1800 are neither numerous nor important, the points of difference being slight, and generally caused by the alteration or "tooling" of some die which had already seen service at the mint.

The type remains the same and even the measurements approach so closely to each other as to make it difficult to distinguish the different varieties. Perhaps the most noticeable feature of the cents of this year is the peculiar tendency manifested by the reverse dies to break at the fraction.

No. 139.—Obv. *Measurements*: Length of word LIBERTY at the base, $9\frac{1}{4}$; distance from the tip of the nose to the nearest point of the letter Y, 3; distance from the tip of the nose to the lower left point of the letter L, $9\frac{3}{4}$; length of date through centre, $4\frac{1}{2}$; distance from the figure 1 to the lowest curl, $\frac{5}{8}$ Upon this obverse the letters E and R and sometimes the T are very weakly impressed, owing to a crack in the reverse die directly opposite those letters. The letter R stands very close to the hair but does not touch. This die was cut over an obverse die of 1798, the figure 8 of the date showing part of 7, while the two ciphers show behind them the 9 and 8, somewhat faintly, it is true, but still with sufficient distinctness to permit their detection by aid of a glass. The date is curved and evenly spaced; the upper right corner of the figure 1 is beneath the shoulder; the last cipher stands quite close to the bust.

Rev.—*Rev. A.*—Upon this reverse there will be found 19 leaves and 5 berries on the right branch of the wreath and 16 leaves and 5 berries on the left. The die was badly broken, the cracks showing themselves as follows: Between the letters R and I of AMERICA, through the lower part of C to the left foot A; from the border milling above the letter C, passing through the centre of the final A, nearly obliterating the fraction, thence passing upward, just touching the end of the right stem, to the wreath, thence through the letter E of UNITED to the border milling beyond; again from the letter N of CENT through the O of ONE to the border, passing through the letters S and T of STATES; the letters STAT are connected by still another break. *Measurements:* Distance from the highest leaf on the right branch of the wreath to the top of the letter O in OF, $3\frac{3}{4}$; distance from the same point to the top of the letter A of STATES, $4\frac{3}{4}$; length of wreath stems from point of union to terminus, right stem: $2\frac{1}{2}$, left stem: $2\frac{1}{2}$; distance between the ribbon ends, $4\frac{1}{4}$. R^5.

No. 140.—Obv. Same as No. 139.

Rev.—*Rev. B.*—Upon this reverse all the letters present ragged edges; the letters AME of AMERICA are connected at the base; there is a lump beneath the letter I of AMERICA; a crack extends through the first cipher of the fraction upward to the left ribbon. *Measurements:* Same as those upon Rev. A. R^4.

No. 141.—Obv. *Measurements:* Length of word LIBERTY at the base, $9\frac{1}{2}$; distance from the tip of the nose to the lower left point of the letter L, $9\frac{3}{4}$; length of date, $4\frac{3}{4}$; distance from the figure 1 to the lowest curl, $\frac{1}{2}$. This die was cut over a die of 1799, the figures 7 and 9 showing plainly beneath the 8 and the first 0, while beneath the final 0 a very faint trace of the 9 can be seen. The date is curved and evenly spaced; the final 0 is not so close to the bust as on No. 139. The letter R is distant from the hair. This die, though designed for a cent of 1799, was never brought into use.

No. 141.

Rev. C.

Rev.—*Rev. C.*—The letters are all very clearly defined; the M and E of AMERICA connect at the base; the dividing line of the fraction has a decided slope to the right. *Measurements:* Same as No. 1. R[1]. On some specimens of this reverse a crack appears, beginning at the centre of the letter I of AMERICA, passing through the final C, the right ribbon, the dividing line of the fraction and the figure 1 of the denominator, to the border milling opposite the letter U of UNITED. Specimens showing these cracks are decidedly rare.

No. 142.—Obv. Same as No. 141.

Rev.—*Rev. D.*—Upon this reverse there is a die-crack beginning at the final 0 of the fraction, passing upward through the dividing line and left ribbon, touching the base of the letter U of UNITED, thence through the N to the border milling beyond. *Measurements:* Same as No. 139. R[1]. [illegible]

No. 143.—Obv. *Measurements:* Length of word LIBERTY at the base, $9\frac{1}{2}$; distance from the tip of the nose to the nearest point of the letter Y, $3\frac{1}{2}$; distance from the tip of the nose to the lower left point of the letter L, $9\frac{3}{4}$; distance between the hair and the letter R, $\frac{1}{8}$; length of date, $4\frac{2}{3}$. This obverse was cut over a partly-finished die, made during the last years of the preceding century, the date reading 179, being so left that it might be filled out as occasion required. The letter L is below the line of its fellows, and nearer to the I than usual; the date is slightly curved; the figure 8 shows very slight traces of the 7 beneath it, while the 9 is plainly to be seen beneath the first 0, the final 0 leans toward its companion.

Rev.—*Rev. E.*—This reverse exhibits a slight crack beginning at the base of the final A of AMERICA, extending through the dividing line of the fraction, barely touching the figure 1 of the denominator, to the border milling opposite the letter U of UNITED. The border milling is broken from a point near the letter C of AMERICA to a point below the fraction. *Measurements*: Same as No. 139. R¹.

No. 144.—Obv. *Measurements*: Length of word LIBERTY at the base, 9⅛; distance from the tip of the nose to the nearest point of the letter Y, 3¼; distance from the tip of the nose to the lower left point of the letter L, 10; length of date, 4¾. The date touches the border milling, and is also nearer the bust than on No. 143; the figure 7 shows itself more distinctly beneath the 8 than on No. 143.

Rev.—*Rev. E.*—R¹.

No. 145.—Obv. Same as No. 144.

Rev.—*Rev. F.*—Upon this die a slight crack, beginning at the left of the final S of STATES, passes through the letter E to the border milling. *Measurements*: Same as No. 139. R¹.

No. 146.—Obv. *Measurements*: Length of word LIBERTY at the base, 9¼; distance from the tip of the nose to the nearest point of the letter Y, 3; distance from the tip of the nose to the lower left point of the letter L, 9⅔; length of date, 5. Upon this obverse the letter L is nearer to the I than upon any of the preceding varieties. This die exhibits several important defects; it is broken from a point at the border to the left of the letter B, the crack extending downward through the hair to the base of E. The date is unevenly curved, well spaced and fully formed, but the figures 1 and 8 are long and inclined too much toward the 0; the top of the 1 is very close to the lowest curl. From the centre of the first 0 an irregular, raised lump extends to the border below the final 0, a similar defect being seen below the end of the hair ribbon to the left.

Rev.—*Rev. G.*—The letters upon this die all exhibit slight defects, principally in the form of scratches on their margins, the most noticeable being on the letters N, T and D of UNITED. A small dot, about the size of a period, is to be seen just above the point of the highest leaf on the left branch of the wreath. *Measurements*: Same as No. 139. R¹.

No. 147.

Rev. II.

No. 147.—Obv. Length of word LIBERTY at the base, 9; distance from the tip of the nose to the nearest point of the letter Y, $3\frac{1}{3}$; distance from the tip of the nose to the lower left point of the letter L, $9\frac{3}{4}$; length of date, 5. The letters ERTY touch the border (~~not~~ so represented in our illustration), the letters are evenly spaced and correctly formed, with the exception of the Y, which has the left end of the stand missing. The date is curved, perfectly formed and evenly spaced.

Rev.—*Rev. II.*—This die exhibits three cracks, one beginning at the upper part of the letter I of AMERICA, extending through the centre of the letters CA, downward to the final 0 of the fraction; another from the left ribbon directly downward, touching the figure 1 of the denominator; another still, a very slight crack, from the end of the right ribbon to the top of the final A of AMERICA. *Measurements*: Same as No. 139. R[5].

No. 148.—Obv. *Measurements*: Length of word LIBERTY at the base, 9; distance from the tip of the nose to the nearest point of the letter Y, $3\frac{1}{3}$; distance from the tip of the nose to the lower left point of the letter L, $9\frac{2}{3}$; length of date, $4\frac{3}{4}$. The figure 1 is very close to the lowest curl; both ciphers are unfinished at base, being mere outlines; particularly the final one.

Rev.—*Rev. I.*—The letter C of CENT is imperfectly formed. *Measurements*: Same as No. 139, with the exception of the length of the wreath stems, the right stem being $2\frac{1}{4}$, the left 2. R[1].

No. 149.—Obv. Similar to No. 148. The ciphers are perfect at the base although the lines are very thin.

Rev.—*Rev. J.*—This die presents a crack beginning at the border above the F in OF and extending to the top of that letter; another beginning at the upper right-hand corner of the letter E of UNITED, touches the D and extends upward to the border at a point midway between that letter and the first S of STATES; another still, begins at the border between the letters S and T of STATES, touching the former and extending to the pair of leaves beneath. *Measurements*: Same as No. 139. R[1].

No. 150.—Obv. This is from the same die as No. 149, but after it had been broken and tooled. The crack begins at the hair, back of the shoulder, and extends to the border on the left. The letters B and R have been tooled and are misshapen, and the same is true with both ciphers in the date.

Rev.—*Rev. K.*—The left down-stroke of the crosslet of the first T of STATES is double; a scratch crosses the right ribbon almost in a line with the dividing line of the fraction. *Measurements*: Same as No. 139. The planchets upon which Nos. 148, 149 and 150 were struck are broader than others of the cents of this year. These numbers may be also identified by the border milling on their reverses, which is much longer than on other varieties. R[1].

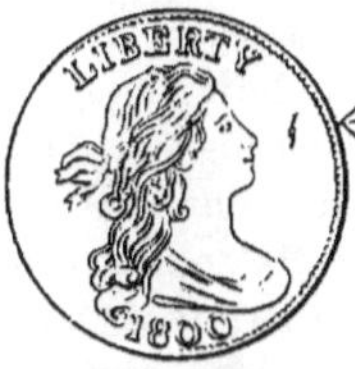

No. 151.

No. 151.—Obv. *Measurements*: Length of word LIBERTY at the base, 9; distance from the tip of the nose to the nearest point of the letter Y, $3\frac{1}{8}$; distance from the tip of the nose to the lower left point of the letter L, $9\frac{3}{8}$; length of date, 5; distance from the figure 8 to the lowest curl, 1. The date touches the border milling, which is very indistinct. The figure 1 touches the top of the lowest curl. The final cipher is quite near to the bust The figures of the date are well formed and evenly spaced, but are all rendered indistinct at their bases by a depression in the die at this point, giving a raised surface to the planchet.

Rev.—*Rev. L.*—This reverse is marked in so peculiar a manner as to render its identification the matter of a glance. The date and a portion of the bust occur incused beneath the impression from the reverse die. The date, 1800, is always found extending from the right crosslet of the second T of STATES through the space between the final S and the O in OF. Several theories have been advanced to explain this peculiarity, none of which seem sufficiently satisfactory to be worthy of mention. The measurements are the same as those of *Rev. A.* R^{1}.

No. 152.—Obv. *Measurements*: Length of word LIBERTY at the base, $9\frac{1}{4}$; distance from the tip of the nose to the nearest point of the letter Y, $3\frac{1}{3}$; distance from the tip of the nose to the lower left point of the letter L, $0\frac{3}{4}$; length of date, 5. The date is widely spaced, the figures well formed and curved. The figure 1 stands equi-distant between the hair and the border milling, as does the final 0 in reference to the milling and the bust.

Rev.—*Rev. M.*—The peculiarities of this reverse are second only to *Rev. L.* The cross stroke of the letter T of UNITED is very uneven; the letters M and E of AMERICA connect at the base; upon the upper left hand corner of the letter R is a small lump. A triangular break in the die shows itself beneath the first 0 of the fraction. From the apex of this triangular break a crack extends through the 0, touching the top of its fellow, crossing the ribbon and extending along the bases of the letters A and C of AMERICA, through the centre of I to the milled border beyond. Upon some specimens another crack shows itself, beginning at a point on the left of the dividing line, touching the ribbon end and extending through the lower corner of the letter U of UNITED to the border milling. The measurements of this reverse are the same as *Rev. A.* R^{1}. Upon some specimens of this combination a small lump, about the size of a period, shows itself in the field upon the obverse, between the neck and the border. There is also a die-crack extending from the hair to the border milling. On the reverse the crack in the die is not so prominent, being visible only from the top of the final 0 of the fraction to the letter E of AMERICA.

No. 153.—Obv. *Measurements*: Length of word LIBERTY at the

base, 9; distance from the tip of the nose to the nearest point of the letter Y, $3\frac{1}{4}$; distance from the tip of the nose to the lower left point of the letter L, $9\frac{2}{3}$; length of date, 5. The date is curved, the figures are evenly spaced and stand midway between the bust and the border. A die-crack, beginning at the letter Y, extends downward to the border opposite the chin.

Rev.—*Rev. M.* When found combined with this obverse, *Rev. M* does not show the cracks mentioned in its description. R[1].

No. 154.—Obv. *Measurements*: Length of word LIBERTY at the base, 9; distance from the tip of the nose to the nearest point of the letter Y, $3\frac{1}{3}$; distance from the tip of the nose to the lower left point of the letter L, $9\frac{2}{3}$; length of date, $4\frac{3}{4}$. The figures of the date are perfectly formed. A die-crack commences at the top of the letter T, passing over the Y to a varying distance, on some specimens continuing around the border to the bust.

Rev.—*Rev. M.*—When found combined with this obverse, *Rev. M* does not show the cracks mentioned in its description. R[1].

No. 155.—Obv. *Measurements*: Length of word LIBERTY at the base, $9\frac{1}{4}$; distance from the tip of the nose to the nearest point of the letter Y, 3; distance from the tip of the nose to the lower left point of the letter L, $9\frac{2}{3}$; length of date, $4\frac{2}{3}$. The figures of the date are well formed and stand almost straight, the 1 only being slightly above the line; the bases of the figures just touch the border milling.

Rev.—*Rev. N.* This reverse is marked by a die-crack beginning at the top of the first A of AMERICA, passing along the tops of the letters M and E, thence downward through the other letters, terminating at a point on the left of the final A just below its cross-stroke. The measurements of this reverse are the same as *Rev. A.* R[5].

With No. 155 terminates the description of the cents of the year 1800. The issue is said to have been greater than that of any previous year, yet we are unable to discover the actual number struck. They are common enough, with the exception of the varieties noted, in ordinary condition, but the copper was very soft, and to find perfectly preserved specimens is a very difficult thing.

1801.

The cents of the year 1801 continued to follow the type of the years immediately preceding, and are marked by bad execution and stupid blunders in legend and fraction. No alteration of the dies of the year 1800 seems to have been attempted. Certainly the standard of artistic skill at the mint during the year 1801 must have been very low.

No. 156.—Obv. *Measurements:* Length of word LIBERTY at the base, 9; distance from the tip of the nose to the nearest point of the letter Y, $3\frac{1}{8}$; distance from the tip of the nose to the lower left point of the letter L, $9\frac{3}{4}$; length of date through the centre, $4\frac{1}{4}$. The letter E is unusually large and stands a little below the line of its fellows; the date is curved and evenly spaced. The first 1 is well formed, but the final 1 is imperfect at the top. The 8 is below the line of the other figures and inclines toward the 0; there is a short perpendicular dash to the right of the final 1.

Rev.—*Rev. A.*—This is the most strongly marked reverse of the cents of this year since it is the most badly blundered. The word *United* is expressed thus: IINITED. This seems to have been done intentionally, and the explanation is believed to lie in the loss of the U punch when making the die and the adoption of the clumsy substitute II in its place. Next we have the wreath, of which the left stem is missing; but the most noticeable blunder is the substitution of a 0 for the figure 1 of the denominator, making the fraction read $\frac{1}{000}$. The letter M of AMERICA is double struck and of peculiar shape. The N, both of UNITED and CENT, is also of peculiar shape on almost all varieties of the cents of this year. The lowest leaf on the inside of the left branch of the wreath is very close to the letter C of CENT, but does not touch. *Measurements*: Length of fraction, $3\frac{1}{4}$; distance between OF and the first A of AMERICA at the top, $2\frac{3}{8}$. R[5]. On some specimens of this reverse a die-crack appears, beginning at the top of the first 0 of the denominator—the one substituted for the figure 1—extending to the left, through the ribbon, along the base of the IIN of IINITED, thence through the upper part of the I to the border milling beyond. Generally a 2d break above this.

No. 157.—Obv. Same as No. 156.

Rev.—*Rev. B.*—The lowest leaf on the inside of the left branch of the wreath just touches the letter C of CENT. The fraction reads $\frac{1}{000}$; the ciphers are very close together. *Measurements*: The word ONE stands $1\frac{1}{4}$ above CENT; distance between the letter D of UNITED and the first S of STATES at the base, $2\frac{1}{2}$; distance between OF and the first A of AMERICA at the top, $2\frac{1}{3}$; length of AMERICA at base, $9\frac{1}{4}$; distance from the tip of the highest leaf on the right branch of the wreath to the top of the letter O in OF, $3\frac{1}{2}$; length of wreath stems from point of union to terminus, right stem: $2\frac{2}{3}$, left stem: 3; distance between the ribbon ends, $4\frac{1}{2}$; length of fraction, $2\frac{3}{4}$. R⁵. On some specimens of this reverse a die-crack appears, beginning above the letter A of STATES, extending through the base of the first T to the tip of the lower leaf of the terminal pair on the right branch of the wreath. Or clear across To rim between F and A.

No. 158. Rev. C.

No. 158.—Obv. *Measurements*: Length of word LIBERTY at the base, $8\frac{3}{4}$; distance from the tip of the nose to the nearest point of the letter Y, $3\frac{1}{4}$; distance from the tip of the nose to the lower left point of the letter L, $9\frac{1}{2}$; length of date through the centre, 4. This is another strongly marked variety. The stand of the letter Y is missing on the left. The die is broken at the border above the letter I, the crack extending through IBERT on some specimens, through IB RTY on others. On other specimens still, there is a die-crack extending from the border to the bust, $4\frac{1}{4}$ in length. The date is slightly curved, the tops of the figures 1 being blunt and the 8 and the 0 very close together.

Rev.—*Rev. C.*—The lowest leaf on the inside of the left branch of the wreath is very close to the letter C of CENT, but does not touch as represented in our illustration. The fraction reads $\frac{1}{000}$, but differs from *Revs. A* and *B* in appearance, the ciphers being round and regular. The left wreath stem terminates in a sharp point. *Measurements*: The word ONE stands 1 above CENT; distance between the letter D of UNITED and the first A of STATES at base, 2$\frac{3}{8}$; distance between OF and the first A of AMERICA at top, 2$\frac{1}{2}$; length of wreath stems from point of union to terminus, right stem: 2$\frac{3}{4}$, left stem: 3$\frac{1}{8}$; distance between the ribbon ends, 4. R^1.

No. 159.—Obv. *Measurements*: Length of word LIBERTY at the base, 9$\frac{3}{8}$; distance from the tip of the nose to the nearest point of the letter Y, 3$\frac{1}{8}$; distance from the tip of the nose to the lower left point of the letter L, 9$\frac{1}{2}$; length of date, 4. The first 1 of the date is blunt on top; the positions of the figures are the same as No. 156.

Rev.—*Rev. D.*—The lowest leaf on the inside of the left branch of the wreath is more distant from the letter C than on *Rev. C*; the letter T of CENT stands slightly above the line of its fellows. The fraction is from the same punch as *Revs. B* and *C*, but shows the figure 1 cut over the first 0 of the denominator, still leaving the cipher perfectly distinct. *Measurements*: Distance from the letter D of UNITED to the first S of STATES at base, 2$\frac{1}{2}$; distance from the letter F in OF to the first A of AMERICA, 2$\frac{1}{2}$; length of wreath stems from point of union to terminus, right stem: 3, left stem: 3; space between the ribbon ends, 4$\frac{1}{4}$. On some specimens of this reverse the die is found cracked on the border above the letters STAT. R^1.

No. 160.—Obv. *Measurements*: Length of word LIBERTY at the base, 9; distance from the tip of the nose to the nearest point of the letter Y, 3$\frac{1}{8}$; distance from the tip of the nose to the lower left point of the letter L, 9$\frac{3}{8}$. The date is divided 1 80 1, as on No. 158.

Rev.—*Rev. E.*—The lowest leaf on the inside of the left branch of the wreath touches the letter C. The letter T of CENT is slightly above the line of its fellows. The numerator of the fraction is closer to the knot than on any of the preceding varieties. The word OF is usually found weakly struck. *Measurements*: Distance between ONE and CENT, 1$\frac{1}{4}$; distance from the letter D of UNITED to the first S of STATES, at base, 2$\frac{1}{8}$; distance between the letter F in OF and the first A of AMERICA, 2; length of wreath stems from point of union to terminus, right stem: 2$\frac{3}{4}$, left stem: 2$\frac{3}{4}$; space between the ribbon ends, 4$\frac{1}{4}$; length of denominator, 2$\frac{1}{4}$. R^1.

No. 161.—Obv. *Measurements*: Length of word LIBERTY at the base, 9½; distance from the tip of the nose to the nearest point of the letter Y, 3½; distance from the tip of the nose to the lower left point of the letter L, 10; length of date through the centre, 4¼. This die seems to have been formed from a scaly piece of steel, causing the impression to present a peculiar appearance. Four wavy lines, almost parallel, appear in front of the head, the lower and largest one beginning at the letter E and extending downward through the hair and forehead, thence sloping toward the border milling to a point directly opposite the chin; the upper one touches the base of the letters TY and extends to the border milling. An attempt seems to have been made to polish this portion of the die, resulting in the partial obliteration of the letters RTY, and leaving the face in unusually high relief. The first 1 of the date is properly formed, while the final 1 is blunt and the 8 a little higher than the other figures.

Rev.—*Rev. F.*—The lowest leaf on the inside of the left branch of the wreath touches the letter C. Only upon this reverse is the letter N properly formed in each instance of its occurrence. The final A of AMERICA is closer to the ribbon than on any other variety. The denominator of the fraction is evenly spaced and stands considerably below the dividing line. *Measurements*: Distance between the letter D of UNITED and the first S of STATES, 2; distance between the letter F in OF and the first A of AMERICA, 1⅞; length of word AMERICA at base, 10; length of wreath stems from point of union to terminus, right stem: 2⅜, left stem: 2½; space between the ribbon ends, 4⅓; length of denominator, 2⅔. A die-crack shows itself beginning at the base of the letters CA of AMERICA and extending to the final 0 of the fraction. R[1]. *Also without break*

No. 162.—Obv. Same as No. 158, but struck previous to the breaking of the die.

Rev.—*Rev. G.*—The letters N and T of CENT connect at the top. There is a small point near the base of the first S of STATES. The denominator of the fraction is separated thus—1 00; the dividing line does not extend above the final 0. *Measurements*: Distance between the letter D of UNITED and the first S of STATES, at the base, 1¾; distance from the letter F in OF to the first A in AMERICA, 3; distance

8 [illegible handwriting]

between the words ONE and CENT, 1; length of wreath stems from

No. 162. Rev. G.

point of union to terminus, right stem: $2\frac{3}{4}$, left stem: $2\frac{3}{4}$; space between the ribbon ends, $4\frac{1}{4}$; length of denominator, $2\frac{1}{2}$. R^5.

No. 163.—Obv. *Measurements:* Length of word LIBERTY at the base, $8\frac{2}{3}$; distance from the tip of the nose to the nearest point of the letter Y, $3\frac{1}{4}$; distance from the tip of the nose to the lower left point of the letter L, $9\frac{2}{3}$; length of date, 4. The figures of the date are evenly spaced, both the first and the final 1 being blunt on top.

Rev.—*Rev. H.*—The final A of AMERICA is not quite so close to the ribbon as on *Rev. G.* The numerator of the fraction is closer to the knot than on any other reverse, while the denominator is separated as on *Rev. G.* *Measurements:* Distance between the letter D of UNITED and the first S of STATES at the base, $2\frac{5}{8}$; distance between the letter F in OF and the first A of AMERICA, $2\frac{1}{2}$; length of wreath stems from point of union to terminus, right stem: 3; left stem: 3; space between the ribbon ends, 4; length of denominator, $2\frac{2}{3}$. On some specimens of this reverse a die-crack shows itself at the border milling above the letter F in OF and also above the letters AME of AMERICA. R^1.

With No. 163 terminates the description of the cents of the year 1801. The mint records state the number coined at 1,362,837. They are quite common in an ordinary or worn condition, but decidedly hard to obtain well preserved or in an uncirculated state. The strongly marked character of the points of difference between the varying dies, renders the selection and arrangement of the varieties easier than is the case with the cents of some of the preceding years.

1802.

The cents of 1802 exhibit no alteration from the type of the preceding years, nor is there much artistic improvement manifested. We find the same blundering and careless workmanship and the same disregard for accuracy, particularly shown in the continued use of the old $\frac{1}{000}$ die (*Rev. C*, 1801). One marked feature is the uniformity in the length of the date, maintained upon every variety of obverse die throughout the year.

No. 164.

No. 164.—Obv. *Measurements*: Length of word LIBERTY at the base, $8\frac{3}{4}$; distance from the tip of the nose to the nearest point of the letter Y, 3; distance from the tip of the nose to the lower left point of the letter L, $9\frac{2}{3}$; length of date at top, $4\frac{1}{3}$. This is also the measurement on every date throughout the year. The figure 1 does not quite touch the hair.

Rev.—*Rev. A.*—This is the same die as *Rev. C*, of the year 1801, to which the reader is referred. R[5].

No. 165.

Rev. B.

No. 165.—Obv. *Measurements*: Length of word LIBERTY at the base, $9\frac{1}{4}$; distance from the tip of the nose to the nearest point of the letter Y, $3\frac{1}{4}$; distance from the tip of the nose to the lower left point of the letter L, 10. The letter I is smaller than its fellows. On some specimens of this obverse a die-crack appears, beginning at a point to the left of the letter R, extending through RTY, from whence it passes in a curved line to the border milling opposite the wreath. (?)

Rev.—*Rev. B.*—The wreath is without stems. The right end of the stand of T is wanting in each instance of that letter's occurrence. *Measurements*: Distance from the letter D of UNITED to the first S of STATES, at base, 2; distance from the last S of STATES to the O in OF, $1\frac{1}{2}$; distance from the F in OF to the first A of AMERICA, $3\frac{1}{8}$; space between the ribbon ends, $4\frac{1}{4}$; space between the numerator and denominator of fraction, $1\frac{1}{4}$. R^1.

No. 166.—Obv. *Measurements:* Length of word LIBERTY at the base, 9; distance from the tip of the nose to the nearest point of the letter Y, $2\frac{1}{2}$; distance from the tip of the nose to the lower left point of the letter L, $9\frac{1}{4}$. (Same as 164)

Rev.—*Rev. C.*—The wreath is without stems. Below the final S of STATES the half of another S appears, touching the top leaf of the right branch of the wreath. The lowest leaf on the left branch of the wreath does not quite touch the letter C of CENT, as on *Rev. B.* Beneath the dividing line of the fraction is a fine line of the same length, which touches the figures of the denominator. The ribbons are longer than on *Rev. B.* *Measurements*: Distance from the letter D of UNITED to the first S of STATES, $2\frac{1}{2}$; distance from the final S of STATES to the O in OF, 2; distance from the F in OF to the first A of AMERICA, 2; space between the ribbon ends, $4\frac{1}{2}$. Upon some specimens of this reverse a die-crack appears above the letters ATE of STATES, and another above the F in OF, extending to the border above the first A of AMERICA. R^1.

No. 167.—Obv. *Measurements*: Length of word LIBERTY at the base, 9; distance from the tip of the nose to the nearest point of the letter Y, 3; distance from the tip of the nose to the lower left point of the letter L, $9\frac{1}{2}$. The letter T has been cut over a Y, the arms of which are still visible extending from the sides to the cross stroke of the T, giving the word somewhat the appearance of LIBERYY.

Rev.—*Rev. D.*—The letters M and E of AMERICA connect at base. The lowest leaf on the left branch of the wreath touches the letter C of CENT. The figures of the fraction are well formed and evenly spaced. *Measurements*: Distance from the letter D of UNITED to the first S of STATES, 1¾; distance from the final S of STATES to the O in OF, 1½; distance from the F in OF to the first A of AMERICA, 2; space between the ribbon ends, 4½; length of wreath stems from point of union to terminus, right stem: 2½, left stem: 2¾. R[1].

No. 168.—Obv. This is the same die as No. 167, but the arms of the Y over which the T is cut are more distinct. One die-crack extends from the upper right corner of the letter T to the border milling, and another, beginning at the top of the letter Y, does the same.

Rev.—*Rev. E.*—The highest leaf on the right branch of the wreath points to the right of the last S of STATES. The lowest leaf on the left branch of the wreath does not touch the C of CENT. The letters NT of CENT connect at the top. The right end of the stand of T is wanting in each instance of that letter's occurrence. The ribbon ends are long, extending to the base of the fraction. The dividing line of the fraction almost touches both ribbons, the numerator is near the knot. *Measurements*: Distance from F in OF to the first A of AMERICA, 3; space between the ribbon ends, 4. On some specimens of this reverse the die is found cracked along the top of STATES to the letter O in OF; the border is broken above ATE and a slight crack extends from the left of the letter M of AMERICA to the border milling above the first A. R[1].

No. 169.—Obv. *Measurements*: Length of word LIBERTY at the base, 9; distance from the tip of the nose to the nearest point of the letter Y, 2½; distance from the tip of the nose to the lower left point of the letter L, 9¼.

Rev.—*Rev. F.*—The lowest leaf on the inside of the right branch of the wreath, does not touch the letter T of CENT. The letters ERICA are connected at the top by a die-crack extending from the upper right corner of E to the top of A. The right end of the stand of T is wanting in each instance of that letter's occurrence. A line extends from the left wreath stem to the letter U of UNITED. *Measurements*: Distance from the letter D of UNITED to the first S of STATES, 2¼; distance from the final S of STATES to the O in OF, 1¾; distance from the F in OF to the first A of AMERICA, 2; space between the ribbon ends, 4½; length of wreath stems from point of union to terminus, right stem: 2⅜; left stem: 3. R[1].

No. 170.—Obv. *Measurements*: Length of word LIBERTY at the base, $8\frac{3}{4}$; distance from the tip of the nose to the nearest point of the letter Y, $3\frac{1}{4}$; distance from the tip of the nose to the lower left point of the letter L, $9\frac{1}{2}$. The figure 1 of the date stands lower and more distant from the hair than on other varieties.

Rev.—*Rev. G.*—The dividing line of the fraction slopes to the right, terminating in a point. A die-crack, beginning at the border, extends through the U of UNITED, thence curving through the bow to the right branch of the wreath. Another crack begins at the border above the final S of STATES and extends directly downward to a point on the opposite border, between the right ribbon and the final A of AMERICA. *Measurements*: Distance from the letter D of UNITED to the first S of STATES, 2; distance from the final S of STATES to the O in OF, $1\frac{2}{3}$; distance from the F in OF to the first A of AMERICA, $1\frac{2}{3}$; space between the ribbon ends, $4\frac{1}{3}$; length of wreath stems from point of union to terminus, right stem: $2\frac{2}{3}$; left stem: $2\frac{1}{2}$. R[5].

No. 171.—Obv. *Measurements*: Length of word LIBERTY at the base, $8\frac{2}{3}$; distance from the tip of the nose to the nearest point of the letter Y, $3\frac{1}{3}$; distance from the tip of the nose to the lower left point of the letter L, $9\frac{1}{2}$.

Rev.—*Rev. H.*—The word ONE stands high in the wreath, and almost touches the leaves. The letter N in each instance of its occurrence is of the same peculiar shape referred to in the description of *Rev. A.* of the cents of 1801 (page 136), and was probably sunk with the same punch. *Measurements*: Distance from the letter D of UNITED to the first S of STATES, $1\frac{3}{4}$; distance from the final S of STATES to the O in OF, $1\frac{1}{2}$; distance from the F in OF to the first A of AMERICA, 2; space between the ribbon ends, $4\frac{1}{4}$; length of wreath stems from point of union to terminus, right stem: $2\frac{1}{2}$; left stem: $2\frac{1}{2}$. A die-crack, beginning at the left of the first S of STATES passes through that letter, touches the tips of two leaves and extends to the border milling above the letter O in OF. R[1].

No. 172.—Obv. *Measurements*: Length of word LIBERTY at the base, 9; distance from the tip of the nose to the nearest point of the letter Y, $3\frac{1}{4}$; distance from the tip of the nose to the lower left point of the letter L, $9\frac{3}{4}$. The top of the figure 1 of the date touches the hair.

Rev.—*Rev. I.*—The lowest leaf on the inside of the left branch of the wreath does not touch the letter C of CENT. *Measurements*: Distance from the letter D of UNITED to the first S of STATES, 2; distance from the final S of STATES to the letter O in OF, 2; distance from the letter F in OF to the first A of AMERICA, 3½; space between the ribbon ends, 4¼; length of wreath stems from point of union to terminus, right stem: 3; left stem: 2⅔. R[1].

On some specimens of this combination the obverse die shows a slight break at the border milling a little below the date; on others a die-crack, beginning at the border milling beneath the 0 of the date passes upward through the figure, and curves across the bust to the border milling on the right. On specimens showing this die-crack, the break at the border is larger than on those which do not. The reverse die in some instances presents a crack, beginning at the middle of the letter E of STATES, passing through the lower part of S through the O in OF to the border milling. This cracked reverse is found in combination with the obverse showing the break first mentioned.

No. 173.—Obv. Same as No. 172. When found in combination with *Rev. J*, this obverse shows the break in the border mentioned above, and, in addition, a die-crack beginning at the base of the letter E, thence curving downward to the right, passing through the head and along the nose to the border milling at a point opposite the chin.

Rev.—*Rev. J.*—The letter N is imperfect in each instance of its occurrence. The left foot of the letter M of AMERICA stands higher than that of the first A. *Measurements*: Distance from the letter D of UNITED to the first S of STATES, 2¼; distance from the final S of STATES to the letter O in OF, 2; distance from the letter F in OF to the first A of AMERICA, 2; space between the ribbon ends, 4⅓; length of wreath stems from point of union to terminus, right stem: 2⅓; left stem: 2⅔. R[1].

No. 174.—Obv. Same as No. 164.

Rev.—*Rev. J.*—When found in combination with this obverse, *Rev. J.* presents a slight die-crack beginning at the left of the top of the letter F in OF, and extending along the top of that letter and AMER of AMERICA. R[1].

No. 175.—Obv. *Measurements*: Length of word LIBERTY at the base 8¾; distance from the tip of the nose to the nearest point of the letter Y, 3½; distance from the tip of the nose to the lower left point of the letter L, 9⅔.

Rev.—*Rev. K.*—The letters AM of AMERICA connect at the base. The right, perpendicular stroke of N touches above. There are only 4 berries on the right branch of the wreath. The two lowest pairs of leaves present defects on their under side. The right wreath stem is much thicker from the middle to the end than from the middle to the knot. The left wreath stem points very much to the left of the letter U of UNITED. The right end of the stand of T is wanting in each instance of that letter's occurrence. *Measurements*: Distance from the letter D of UNITED to the first S of STATES, 2; distance from the final S of STATES to the O in OF, 2; distance from the F in OF to the first A of AMERICA, 1¾; space between the ribbon ends, 4½; length of wreath stems from point of union to terminus, right stem: 2¾; left stem: 3. R[5].

This reverse die is sometimes found in a badly cracked condition. On these cracked specimens the border is broken above the letters STA of STATES, and a crack beginning at the base of the first S, curves upward, and ends at the last S. Another crack beginning at the border milling, between the letters E and S, curves downward through the right branch of the wreath, and passes through the letter I of AMERICA to the border milling beyond. Two smaller cracks unite with this, the first beginning at a point between the letter F in OF and the first A of AMERICA, the other passing through the letter E of AMERICA.

No. 176.—Obv. *Measurements*: Length of word LIBERTY at the base, 9; distance from the tip of the nose to the nearest point of the letter Y, 2¾; distance from the tip of the nose to the lower left point of the letter L, 9¼.

Rev.—*Rev. L.*—There are but 4 berries on the right branch of the wreath. The right end of the stand of T is wanting in each instance of that letter's occurrence. *Measurements*: Distance from the letter D of UNITED to the first S of STATES, 2½; distance from the final S of STATES to the O in OF, 2; distance from the F in OF to the first A of AMERICA, 1¾; space between the ribbon ends, 4⅓; length of wreath stems from point of union to terminus, right stem: 2$\frac{3}{4}$; left stem: 2$\frac{3}{4}$. A die-crack beginning at a point between the letters A and T of STATES, extends downward and crosses the top of the letter N of ONE CENT; from this point one branch continues to the border milling, passing through the first A of AMERICA, while the other extends downward through the E of CENT to the border below the left ribbon. R[1].

No. 177.—Obv. *Measurements*: Length of the word LIBERTY at the base, 9; distance from the tip of the nose to the nearest point of the letter Y, 3; distance from the tip of the nose to the lower left point of the letter L, 9$\frac{1}{4}$.

Rev.—*Rev. L.*—When found combined with this obverse, *Rev. L.* does not present the cracks mentioned in its description. R[1]. On some specimens of this combination the obverse die shows a die-crack beginning at a point at the border milling above R, passing through that letter, touching the forelock, and extending to the border opposite the chin. A very slight crack also passes through the letter E to the hair. NOTE

No. 178.—Obv. Same as No. 166. When found combined with *Rev. K*, this obverse sometimes shows a die-crack beginning at a point on the border, to the left, and passing through the letter T to the highest point of the hair; at others there is a break above the letters TY, and a crack extending from the throat directly to the border milling, on the right. This latter variety is rare.

Rev.—*Rev. K.*—R[1].—R[5].

With No. 178 terminates the description of the cents of the year 1802. The number struck is said to have been 3,435,100. In ordinary condition, none but the varieties noted are at all difficult to obtain, but in a fine or uncirculated state, all varieties command a price.

1803.

The cents of the year 1803, while maintaining the type of the years immediately preceding, still exhibit marked artistic improvement, most of the old, blundered dies of 1801 having been discarded, although in one instance we find $\frac{1}{100}$ cut over $\frac{1}{000}$. The most noticeable peculiarity of the cents of this year lies in the frequent occurrence of a die-crack at the word STATES. Another is the formation of the figure 1 in the date, which, except in a single instance, occurs with a blunt top.

No. 179.—Obv. *Measurements*: Length of word LIBERTY at the base, 8½; distance from the tip of the nose to the nearest point of the letter Y, 3¼; distance from the tip of the nose to the lower left point of the letter L, 9½; length of date at top, 4⅓. Upon this obverse a small lump occurs beneath the chin, touching the throat.

Rev.—*Rev. A.*—The word ONE stands very close to the leaves above. The letters NT of CENT connect at the top. *Measurements*: Distance from the letter D of UNITED to the first S of STATES, and from the letter F in OF to the first A of AMERICA, 2½; distance from the final S of STATES to the O in OF, 2¼; length of wreath stems from point of union to terminus, right stem: 2¾, left stem: 2¾; distance between the ribbon ends, 4¼. The fraction shows the figure 1 cut over the first cipher of the denominator, being from the same punch as *Rev. D*, of the year 1801. R[6].

No. 180.—Obv. *Measurements*: Same as No. 179. The letter T is not so much to the left of the forelock as on No. 179.

Rev.—*Rev. B.*—This is the same die as *Rev. C.* of the year 1802, the description of which we copy.

"The wreath is without stems. Below the final S of STATES the half of another S appears, touching the top leaf of the right branch of the wreath. The lowest leaf on the left branch of the wreath does not quite touch the letter C of CENT, as on *Rev. B* [1802]. Beneath the dividing line of the fraction is a fine line of the same length which touches the figures of the denominator. The ribbons are longer than on *Rev. B* [1802]. *Measurements*: Distance from the letter D of UNITED to the first S of STATES, 2½; distance from the final S of STATES to the O in OF, 2; distance from the F in OF to the first A of AMERICA, 2; space between the ribbon ends, 4½. Upon some specimens of this reverse a die-crack appears above the letters ATE of STATES, and another above the F in OF, extending to the border above the first A of AMERICA." R[1]. Upon some specimens of this combination the obverse die is found broken on the border above the letters

TY, thence extending downward to a point opposite the nose. Another crack beginning at the lowest curl, extends downward through the date to the drapery on the bust.

No. 181.—Obv. Same as No. 179.

Rev.—*Rev. C.*—The lowest, inner leaf on the inside of the right branch of the wreath is united with the base, and touches the tip of the letter T of CENT. The corresponding leaf on the left branch of the wreath touches the letter C. The die is broken at the border along the tops of the letters STA of STATES. The numerator of the fraction stands nearer to the knot than to the dividing line. *Measurements*: Distance from the letter D of UNITED to the first S of STATES, 2½; distance from the final S of STATES to the O in OF, 2; distance from the F in OF to the first A of AMERICA, 2¼; length of wreath stems from point of union to terminus, right stem: 2⅔; left stem: 2⅔; distance between the ribbon ends, 4½. R [1].

No. 182.—Obv. Same as No. 179.

Rev.—*Rev. D*—The figures of the fraction are evenly spaced. The left wreath stem is pointed. A slight defect in the die, caused by the edging tool, extends from the end of the right ribbon through the fraction to the letter U of UNITED. *Measurements*: Distance from the letter D of UNITED to the first S of STATES, 2⅓; distance from the final S of STATES to the O in OF, 1¾; distance from the F in OF to the first A in AMERICA, 2; length of wreath stems from point of union to terminus, right stem: 2⅓; left stem: 2⅓; space between the ribbon ends, 4; length of dividing line of the fraction, 1¼. R [1].

No. 183.—Obv. *Measurements*: Length of word LIBERTY at the base, 8⅔; distance from the tip of the nose to the nearest point of the letter Y, 3⅓; distance from the tip of the nose to the lower left point of the letter L, 9½; length of date at top, 4¼. The figure 1 is more distant from the lowest curl than upon No. 179; the figure 3 touches the bust.

Rev.—*Rev. E.*—The right ~~ribbon~~ stem-end is pointed. The dividing line of the fraction stands at a slight angle, is thick and of medium length. *Measurements*: Distance from the letter D of UNITED to the first S of STATES, 2½; distance from the final S of STATES to the O in OF,

$2\frac{1}{4}$; distance from the F in OF to the first A of AMERICA, 2; length of wreath stems from point of union to terminus, right stem: $3\frac{1}{2}$; left stem, $3\frac{1}{4}$; space between the ribbon ends, $4\frac{1}{2}$; length of dividing line of fraction, 2. All impressions from this die exhibit a crack beginning at the border to the left of the first S of STATES, extending through that letter, touching T, thence curving upward and passing through E. A small defect also appears to the right of the fraction very close to the terminal cipher. R[1]. Upon some specimens an additional die-crack shows itself, beginning at the letters ED of UNITED, passing on to the border to the right of D, thence inward to the left branch of the wreath, thence upward through the terminal leaf to the base of the last S of STATES. Upon other specimens still there is a crack in the obverse die connecting the figure 180 of the date, thence extending to the left. This crack measures $5\frac{1}{2}$ in length.

No. 184.—Obv. *Measurements*: Same as No. 183. The date is less curved than upon that number and is divided thus: 18 03. The figure 3 just touches the bust. Upon this obverse a die-crack appears beginning at the throat and extending downward to the base of the bust in front, thence upward to a point near the border opposite the nose, thus taking somewhat the shape of the letter V.

Rev.—*Rev. F.*—The word ONE stands high in the wreath, but not quite as much so as upon *Rev. A.* *Measurements*: Distance from the letter D of UNITED to the first S of STATES, $1\frac{3}{8}$; distance from the final S of STATES to the O in OF, $1\frac{3}{4}$; distance from the F in OF to the first A of AMERICA, $2\frac{1}{3}$; length of wreath stems from point of union of terminus, right stem: $2\frac{3}{8}$; left stem: $2\frac{5}{8}$; space between the ribbon ends, $4\frac{1}{2}$. Upon all impressions from this die there is a crack, which begins at a point to the left of the first S of STATES, thence branches in three directions, extending through the letters STAT and terminating at the border between the letters T and E. R[6]. This variety has been styled the "Divided Date."

No. 185.—Obv. Divided Date; same as No. 184.

Rev.—*Rev. G.*—There are *six* berries upon the left branch of the wreath, while all other reverses of this date, save *Rev. M*, have but five. The additional berry is on the outside, opposite the first S of STATES. The letter N in each instance of its occurrence is from the same peculiar punch mentioned in our description of *Rev. A*, cents of 1801. *Measurements* : Distance from the letter D of UNITED to the first S of STATES, 2; distance from the final S of STATES to the O in OF, 1½; distance from the F in OF to the first A of AMERICA, 2½; length of wreath stems from point of union to terminus, right stem: 2¾; left stem: 2¾; space between the ribbon ends, 4¼. R^5. Upon some specimens of this combination the obverse die shows a break at the border which connects all the figures of the date, terminating beneath the lowest curl, the entire length of the imperfection being 6¼. Upon this reverse the die is sometimes found cracked between the letter D of UNITED and the first S of STATES, the crack extending to the wreath, thence upward through the highest pair of leaves on the right branch, touching the O in OF and terminating at the border above.

No. 186.—Obv. *Measurements*: Length of word LIBERTY at the base, 8¾; distance from the tip of the nose to the nearest point of the letter, Y 4½; distance from the tip of the nose to the lower left point of the letter L, 9⅓; length of date at top, 4½. The date is divided in a manner similar to No. 184, but in this instance the figure 8 has a greater inclination toward the 0. A break in the die connects the figures 18 with the curl, passing thence to the border, the extreme length of the imperfection being 4.

Rev.—*Rev. H.*—*Measurements* : Distance from the letter D of UNITED to the first S of STATES, 2⅘; distance from the final S of STATES to the O in OF, 2⅔; distance from the F in OF to the first A of AMERICA, 1¾; length of wreath stems from point of union to terminus, right stem: 2⅓; left stem: 2⅔; space between the ribbon ends, 4. R^1.

No. 187.—Obv. *Measurements* : Length of word LIBERTY at base, 9; distance from the tip of the nose to the nearest point of the letter Y, 3⅓; distance from the tip of the nose to the lower left point of the letter L, 9⅘; length of date at top, 4⅘. The stand of the letter Y and a part of that of the T is missing. The date is irregularly spaced and but slightly curved; the figure 3 stands very close to the 0.

Rev.—*Rev. I.*—The letter T is imperfect in each instance of its occurrence. The left wreath stem points to the left foot of the letter N of UNITED. The ribbon ends are unusually short, extending only to the top of the denominator of the fraction. The figures of the fraction are distant from the dividing line. *Measurements*: Distance from the letter D of UNITED to the first S of STATES, $2\frac{1}{3}$; distance from the final S of STATES to the O in OF, 2; distance from the F in OF to the first A of AMERICA, $2\frac{1}{4}$; length of wreath stems from point of union to terminus, right stem: $2\frac{3}{4}$; left stem: $2\frac{3}{4}$. R[1]. Upon some specimens of this reverse a die-crack appears beginning at the border on the left of STATES and connecting the letters ST, thence passing upward, but not touching the letter A. The extreme length of this imperfection is $5\frac{1}{2}$.

No. 188.—Obv. Divided Date; Not same as No. 184. When found in combination with *Rev. J*, this obverse die shows a crack beginning at a point immediately to the left of the figure 8 through which it passes, thence curving upward through the bust to the border beyond.

Rev.—*Rev. J.—Measurements*: Distance from the letter D of UNITED to the first S of STATES, $2\frac{1}{2}$; distance from the final S of STATES to the O in OF, $2\frac{1}{3}$; distance from the F in OF to the first A of AMERIÇA, $1\frac{3}{4}$; length of wreath stems from point of union to terminus, right stem: $2\frac{1}{2}$; left stem: 3; space between the ribbon ends, $4\frac{1}{3}$. This die is badly cracked. It is broken at the border above the letters STA, the break touching only the letter T. The extreme length of this imperfection is $3\frac{1}{2}$. A die-crack beginning at a point on the left of the letter D of UNITED, passes through the letter, thence curving upward through the left branch of the wreath to the border between the letters E and S. At the tip of the highest leaf a branch crack strikes off toward the right, extending through the centre of the letter O in OF to the border beyond. Another slight crack beginning at a point between the letters A and M of AMERICA, extends to the wreath, terminating at a point opposite the top of the letter E in ONE. R[1].

No. 189.—Obv. *Measurements*: Length of word LIBERTY at the base, $8\frac{3}{4}$; distance from the tip of the nose to the nearest point of the letter Y, 3; distance from the tip of the nose to the lower left point of the letter L, 9½ ; length of date at top, 4⅓. The letter L is below the line of its fellows; the letters IB are connected at the top; the date is widely spaced, the figure 3 extends more deeply into the drapery of the bust than upon any other variety. An indentation in the die has produced a raised imperfection, extending outward from the centre of the forehead to an extreme length of 1½. The imperfection, having somewhat the appearance of a horn, has caused this variety to be styled the "Unicorn."

Rev.—*Rev. K.*—This is the same die as *Rev. F*, cents of 1802. When found in this combination a piece is broken off the die at the border above the letters RICA; probably the result of the extension of the crack mentioned in its description. R 1.

No. 190.

No. 190.—Obv. *Measurements*: Length of word LIBERTY at the base, 8¾; distance from the tip of the nose to the nearest point of the letter Y, 3; distance from the tip of the nose to the lower, left point of the letter L, 9½ ; length of date at top, 4. The date is unevenly spaced, the figure 1 being closer to the 8 than the 8 to the 0 or the 0 to the 3; the 1 is distant from the hair and the 3 at a greater distance from the bust than in any of the preceding varieties.

Rev.—*Rev. L.*—The lowest leaf on the inside of the left branch of the wreath does not quite touch the letter C of CENT. The letters NT of CENT connect at top, and stand below the line of CE. The final S of STATES shows the outline of another S a little to the right. There is a small dot at the end of the left wreath stem. The dividing line of the fraction is unusually short. *Measurements*: Distance from the letter D of UNITED to the first S of STATES, 2; distance from the final S of STATES to the O in OF, 1½; distance from the F in OF to the first A of AMERICA, 3¼; length of wreath stems from point of union to terminus, right stem: 2¾; left stem: 2¾; space between the ribbon ends, 4¼; length of dividing line of fraction, 1¼. R¹. This variety, owing to the shortness of the dividing line of the fraction, has been styled the "Short Dash." Upon some specimens a die-crack shows itself beginning at the border between the letter D of UNITED and the first S of STATES, thence curving upward through the wreath, coming very close to the highest leaf, then turning sharply to the right, passing through the wreath and terminating at the border at a point midway between the F in OF and the first A of AMERICA. Specimens exhibiting this crack are decidedly rare.

No. 191.—Obv. *Measurements*: Length of word LIBERTY at the base, 9; distance from the tip of the nose to the nearest point of the letter Y, 3; distance from the tip of the nose to the lower left point of the letter L, 9¾; length of date at top, 4½. The letters RTY are above the line of their fellows, particularly the R. The date is evenly spaced; the figure 3 just touches the bust. A slight die-crack beginning at a point on the right of the date passes through the bust to the border immediately in front.

Rev.—*Rev. I.*—R¹.

No. 192.—Obv. *Measurements*: Length of word LIBERTY at the base, 8⅔; distance from the tip of the nose to the nearest point of the letter Y, 3⅓; distance from the tip of the nose to the lower left point of the letter L, 9⅔; length of date at top, 4¼. The forelock points between the letters T and Y, the figure 3 does not touch the bust.

Rev.—*Rev. M.*—There are *six* berries on the left branch of the wreath. The letters and figures are large and perfectly formed, having evidently been cut from a new set of punches which were also employed upon *Revs. N, O* and *P.* The dividing line of the fraction is short. *Measurements*: Distance from the letter D of UNITED to the first S of STATES, 1⅔; distance from the final S of STATES to the O in OF, 1⅓; distance from the F in OF to the first A of AMERICA, 1⅓: length of wreath stems from point of union to terminus, right stem:

2½; left stem: 2½; space between the ribbon ends, 4⅓; length of the dividing line of fraction, 1¼. R[1]. Upon some specimens of this reverse a die-crack appears, beginning at a point on the border at the left of the first S of STATES, touching the tail of that letter, thence crossing both branches of the wreath and passing upward through the F in OF to the border beyond. Another crack, beginning at the letter A of STATES, passes through that letter, curves upward, touching the tips of both branches of the wreath and the final S of STATES, terminating at the border at a point between that letter and the O in OF. Specimens exhibiting these die-cracks are decidedly rare.

No. 193.—Obv. Same as No. 192.

Rev.—*Rev. N.*—The left wreath stem points to the left foot of the letter N in UNITED. All the letters of the word CENT are connected. *Measurements*: Distance from the letter D of UNITED to the first S of STATES, 1¾; Distance from the final S of STATES to the O in OF, 1½; distance from the F in OF to the first A of AMERICA, 1⅔; length of wreath stems from point of union to terminus, right stem: 2¾; left stem: 3; length of dividing line of the fraction, 1½. A slight die-crack connects the letter D of UNITED at the top with the border above. R[1]. Upon some specimens of this combination the obverse die shows a crack, beginning at the figure 1, passing to the left, curving upward, touching the lowest tip of the ribbon and terminating at the border beyond.

No. 194.—Obv. *Measurements*: Length of word LIBERTY at the base, 9; distance from the tip of the nose to the nearest point of the letter Y, 3¼; distance from the tip of the nose to the lower left point of the letter L, 9½; length of date, 4¼. The date is slightly curved and the figures close; the figure 3 is weak at the base and its top is horizontal instead of sloping, as is usual on cents of this year. A die-crack connecting the two curls below the ear, extends thence to the junction of the neck and bust, and from that point strikes upward to the chin. The peculiar appearance of the figure 3 has earned for this variety the name "Thin 3."

Rev.—*Rev. N.*—When found combined with this obverse, *Rev. N.* presents one die-crack connecting the border and the first S in STATES;

another connecting the tops of the letters TAT. In some instances the border is wanting above these letters. R[1].

No. 195.—Obv. Same as No. 194. When found combined with *Rev. O*, the figure 3 is seen to have been re-cut.

Rev.—*Rev. O.*—The letters N and T of CENT are above the line of their fellows. The T extends into the leaf at its base to a greater distance than on other reverses of this date. *Measurements*: Distance from the letter D of UNITED to the first S of STATES, $1\frac{1}{2}$; distance from the final S of STATES to the O in OF, $1\frac{1}{3}$; distance from the F in OF to the first A of AMERICA, $1\frac{3}{4}$; length of wreath stems from point of union to terminus, right stem: $2\frac{3}{4}$; left stem: $2\frac{3}{4}$; space between the ribbon ends, $4\frac{1}{4}$; length of the dividing line of the fraction, 2. R[1].

No. 196.—Obv. This obverse is so strongly marked as to render measurements unnecessary, the die being badly cracked. One defect begins at a point on the border between the 8 and the 0, passes upward through the shoulder and the highest curl, thence through the ribbon to the border on the left. Another crack beginning at the curl crosses the neck, presenting the appearance of an irregular scar. The date is $4\frac{1}{2}$ in length at the top, the figures are widely separated, the 3 touching the drapery. The peculiar mark on the neck has caused this obverse to be styled the "Scarred Neck." This is the obverse die employed in the well-known "Mint re-strike" of the cent of 1804.

Rev.—*Rev. O.* R[1].

No. 197.—Obv. This obverse, known as the "Large Date," is another strongly marked variety.

The date measures $4\frac{1}{4}$ in length at the top. The figures are taller and stand closer together than usual. The 1 is perfectly formed, which is not the case in any other instance of its occurrence on cents of this date, the tops in all other cases being blunt. The curve of the 3 is unusually full. The 1 touches the hair and the 3 the drapery.

Rev.—*Rev. P.*—The letters ENT of CENT are connected. *Measurements*: Distance from the letter D of UNITED to the first S of STATES,

$2\frac{1}{4}$; distance from the final S of STATES to the O in OF, $1\frac{3}{4}$; distance from the F in OF to the first A of AMERICA, $1\frac{1}{2}$; length of wreath stems from point of union to terminus, right stem : $2\frac{3}{4}$; left stem : $2\frac{3}{4}$; space between the ribbon ends, $4\frac{1}{3}$; length of the dividing line of the fraction, $1\frac{3}{4}$. R[5]. Upon some specimens of this reverse a die-crack beginning at the first S of STATES touches the base of T and the leaf below A, thence extending to E and curving downward to a point between the O of ONE and the leaf on its left. Specimens exhibiting this die-crack are even more difficult to obtain than those without it.

With No. 197 terminates the description of the cents of the year 1803. The number struck is said to have been 2,471,353. There is no difficulty in obtaining finely preserved specimens of the cents of this year.

1804.

No. 198.

Rev. A.

A single pair of dies was employed in the manufacture of the cents of this year, and the high degree of rarity of their impressions renders this cent the most notable issue of the present century. The type is the same as the years preceding.

No. 198.—Obv. The date is $4\frac{1}{2}$ in length through the centre. The figure 1 has a blunt top, but the other figures are well formed. The stand of the 4 on the right is on a line with the crosslet. To the right of the crosslet are two short, perpendicular lines. The 0 is exactly opposite the O in OF on the reverse, a peculiarity occurring only in this cent.

Rev.—*Rev. A.*—There are 5 berries upon either branch of the wreath. A thin line, measuring 1 in length extends obliquely upward from the top of the lowest leaf on the inside of the left branch of the wreath—the one touching the C of CENT. The figures of the fraction are large and well spaced. *Measurements*: Distance from the letter D of UNITED to the first S of STATES, $2\frac{1}{3}$; distance from the final S of STATES to the O in OF, $\frac{3}{4}$; distance from the F in OF to the first A of AMERICA, $1\frac{1}{3}$; length of wreath stems from point of union to terminus, right stem: 3; left stem: 3; space between the ribbon ends, $4\frac{1}{3}$, R^7. Upon some specimens the obverse die is found broken at the border above and touching the letters RTY. Specimens presenting this defect may be classed R^8. Again, specimens occur which in addition to the defect on the obverse, present a similar break on the reverse die at the border, touching the letters MERI of AMERICA and projecting slightly beyond the I toward the C. Specimens exhibiting this double imperfection may be classed with the perfect impressions, R^7.

The high degree of rarity of the cent of 1804, has been recognized for many years. The issue is said to have been 756,838; small in comparison with other years, truly, but still sufficiently large to make it a matter of surprise that this cent should be so rare. As early as 1859, when Dr. M. W. Dickeson published his *American Numismatic Manual*, they were highly prized, and the interest has of late years greatly increased. In the sale of the collection of John F. McCoy, in 1864, an uncirculated impression realized the enormous sum of $32, and in later years uncirculated specimens have changed hands at a much higher price. As is the case with all rarities, the value of the 1804 cent depends entirely upon the state of preservation in which it is found. Still the rarity of this cent cannot be said to equal that of the year 1799, much worn impressions of which date command higher prices than fairly good examples of the 1804.

Like the cent of 1799, the 1804 has been extensively imitated, certain persons connected with the Philadelphia mint even, it is claimed, having assisted in the fraud.

The imitations of the cent of 1804 consist of alterations from cents of 1801, which can not only be readily detected by a glass, but in many instances exhibit that ancient blunder $\frac{1}{000}$ upon the reverse, determining their true character; occasionally plugged pieces, specimens of any common variety of the draped bust of the nineteenth century with the figure 4 inserted, and lastly the *soi-disant* "Mint Re-strike," which demands a careful description.

The Mint Re-strike.—This singular example of the low moral tone of some of our public officials made its appearance about the year 1860, a time when the craze for cent collecting may be said to have reached high-water mark. Although generally referred to by the name we have given it, this nondescript was in no sense a re-strike, but a thing of shreds and patches, manufactured for the sole purpose of supplying coin dealers with a cent bearing the mystic figures 1804 which they could sell to young and ignorant collectors at a high price.

The obverse die is an alteration of No. 196, while the reverse is one of the dies employed in the year 1818. When resuscitated, the obverse die was probably badly corroded, and an attempt to remove the corrosion left it very rough, which caused the imperfections noticeable all over the obverse of the piece. The figures 180 were re-cut and a 4 cut over the 3, with traces of the older figure remaining visible beneath. The letters were also re-cut and present an abnormally sharp appearance, and two new cracks appear, branching to the right and left of those mentioned in the description of the die.

Of course, the reverse bears no resemblance whatever to that of the genuine cent, but it has also undergone the sharpening process. The dash found beneath the word CENT upon the issues of 1818 was obliterated.

Certainly no collector worthy of the name should be deceived by this wretched fraud.

1805.

The cents of the year 1805 are of the same type as the years preceding, and the number of varieties is limited to three, although *five* are claimed by Dr. Dickeson and by another writer, *four*. There are no marked peculiarities offered by the cents of this year.

No. 199.—Obv. *Measurements*: Length of word LIBERTY at the base, 9; distance from the tip of the nose to the nearest point of the letter L, 9½; length of date at the top, 4¼. The figure 1 is blunt at the top and the 5 just touches the bust. The outlines of another 5 are to be seen a little to the right of the figure.

Rev.—*Rev. A.*—There are five berries upon either branch of the wreath. The inner leaf on the right branch of the wreath just touches the T of CENT. The denominator of the fraction is slightly curved and the figures are unusually small. *Measurements*: Distance from the letter D of UNITED to the first S of STATES, 2⅓; distance from the final S of STATES to the O in OF, 1½; distance from the F in OF to the first A of AMERICA, 2¼; length of denominator of the fraction, 2¾; length of wreath stems from point of union to terminus, right stem: 2⅔, left stem: 2¾. R^2.

No. 200.—Obv. This is the same die as No. 199, but all traces of the additional 5 have been removed.

Rev.—*Rev. B.*—The letters N and T are connected at the top. The inner leaf on the right branch of the wreath is more distant from the T than on No. 199. The left branch of the wreath and the stem of the right branch are disconnected from the knot. The figures of the denominator of the fraction are in a straight line. *Measurements*: Distance from the final S of STATES to the O in OF, 1¾; distance from the F in OF to the first A of AMERICA, 3; length of denominator of the fraction, 2⅝; length of wreath stems from point of union to terminus, right stem: 2⅓, left stem: 3. R^3.

No. 201.—Obv. *Measurements*: Length of word LIBERTY at the base, 9⅓; distance from the tip of the nose to the nearest point of the letter Y, 3; distance from the tip of the nose to the lower left point of the letter L, 9⅝; length of date at top, 4½. The figure 1 is perfectly

No. 201.

formed; the top of the 5 does not quite touch the bust. The tops of the letters touch the border. There is an oblique scratch extending from the lower left ribbon of the band to the hair, above the highest curl on the left. In front of the bust are four minute points.

Rev.—*Rev. B.* R².

The cents of 1805 are not common, even in poor condition, and decidedly scarce well preserved. Frequently they are found covered with a beautiful olive green patination and sometimes quite black. No. 200 can only be termed scarce. The number struck is said to have been 941,116.

1806.

But one pair of dies were used in striking the cents of the year 1806. Dr. Dickeson's variety from the altered die of 1805, and the other that he mentioned with $\frac{1}{000}$ upon the reverse, have never been verified; the auction cataloguer's distinctions cannot be accepted, and the claim for four dies (undescribed) made by another writer, remains yet to be proved. Scarce in ordinary condition, the cents of 1806, in the very fine or uncirculated state may be ranked among the rarest of the rare. The number struck is said to have been only 348, 000.

No. 202.—Obv. *Measurements*: Length of word LIBERTY at the base, 9; distance from the tip of the nose to the nearest point of the letter Y, 3¼; distance from the tip of the nose to the lower left point of the

No. 202.

letter L, $9\frac{3}{4}$; length of date, $5\frac{1}{4}$. The letters I and B are small, the latter being below the line. The figures of the date are unusually perfect, the 6 just touches the bust.

Rev. Same as *Rev. B* of the cents of 1805. R³.

1807

The cents of the year 1807 maintain the style of the preceding years, and are notable as the last of the "Draped Bust" type, begun in the year 1796. There are five varieties of the cents of 1807, the most remarkable of which has the figure 7 in the date cut over the 6 of the obverse die employed during the year 1806.

No. 203.

No. 203.—Obv. This obverse die is the same as No. 202, but in this instance has the figure 7 cut over the 6, the latter remaining distinctly visible beneath.

Rev.—*Rev. A.*—The left wreath stem terminates in a point. The figures of the fraction are small. The loops of the bow do not connect with the branches below. *Measurements*: Distance from the letter D of UNITED to the first S of STATES, 1¾; distance from the final S of STATES to the O in OF, 1½; distance from the F in OF to the first A of AMERICA, 2; length of denominator of the fraction, 2½; length of wreath stems from point of union to terminus, right stem: 2⅓, left stem: 3; space between the ribbon ends, 4¼. A die-crack beginning at the lowest leaf on the right branch of the wreath passes through the C of AMERICA to the border. R[1].

No. 204.

No. 204.—Obv. *Measurements*: Length of word LIBERTY at the base, 9¼; distance from the tip of the nose to the nearest point of the letter Y, 3; distance from the tip of the nose to the lower left point of the letter L, 9¾; length of date at base, 4½. The figure 1 is blunt at the top. The remaining figures are well formed and all are equally spaced.

Rev.—*Rev. B.*—The letters of the word CENT all stand at different angles; the lowest leaf on the left branch of the wreath does not touch the C. The dividing line of the fraction is continued through the ribbon to the top of the final A of AMERICA. The letters STA of STATES are faintly impressed. *Measurements*: Distance from the letter D of UNITED to the first S of STATES, 3¼; distance from the final S of STATES to the O in OF, 1⅜; distance from the F in OF to the first A of AMERICA, 2¼; length of denominator of the fraction, 2¾; length of wreath stems from point of union to terminus, right stem: 2¾, left stem: 2⅜; space between the ribbons ends, 4⅓. R[2].

No. 205.—Obv. Same as No 204, but struck after the die had been

Not [illegible]

injured—perhaps by sharpening. There is a prominent flaw extending from the back of the head to the border on the left, and upon some specimens a line is seen extending from the nose to the border on the right.

Rev.—*Rev. A.*—When found in combination with this obverse, *Rev. A* does not exhibit the small die-crack mentioned in its description. R[1].

No. 206.—Obv. Same as No. 204, and struck while the die was yet perfect.

Rev.—*Rev. C.*—The letters NT of CENT are connected. The figures of the fraction are unusually large. *Measurements:* Distance from the letter D of UNITED to the first S of STATES, 2¼; distance from the final S of STATES to the O in OF, 1¾: distance from the F in OF, to the first A of AMERICA, 1½; length of wreath stems from point of union to terminus, right stem: 2¾; left stem: 2¾; space between the ribbon ends, 4⅓; length of dividing line of fraction, 1¾. R[3].

No. 207.—Obv. *Measurements*: Length of word LIBERTY at the base, 9½; distance from the tip of the nose to the nearest point of the letter Y, 3⅓; distance from the tip of the nose to the nearest point of the letter L, 9¾; length of date at base, 4⅓. The letters IB are smaller and above the line of their fellows.

Rev.—*Rev. C.*—R[1].

In ordinary condition the cents of 1807 are easily obtained, but in fine preservation or uncirculated they are rare. The number struck is said to have been 727,221.

1808.

The year 1808 marks an entire change in the type of the cent.

Upon the obverse the draped bust gives place to a head of Liberty of a wholly different and far more artistic character, and now, for the first time, facing to the left. The features are those of a young female, and are regular and expressive. A plain ribbon secures the hair above the forehead, beneath which it falls in graceful curls. Upon the ribbon is inscribed the word LIBERTY. This year marks also the first appearance of stars, of which there are 7 to the left, in front of the head, and 6 to the right, behind. The date is under the bust, which is much shorter than on the cents of the preceding type.

This obverse is usually styled the "Turban Head," one of those strange misnomers so common among our early collectors, for, as will be seen, no turban exists. It is generally conceded that this design is by far the most beautiful that has ever appeared upon the cents of the United States, and its early abandonment, which occurred in the year 1816, is certainly a matter of regret.

The strange inaccuracy of Dr. Dickeson in many of his statements is strikingly manifest in his description of the cents of this year, where he claims that Draped Bust cents bearing the date 1808 were issued during the early portions of the year, an assertion which is entirely false. There was but one obverse die employed in striking the cents of 1808.

The reverse of the cents of 1808 is likewise of a different character. The lettering is larger and beneath the word CENT a short dash now makes its appearance to remain until the year 1839. The wreath stems are connected at the top and the fraction disappears to return no more.

No. 208.—Obv. Head of Liberty to left, the hair confined by a ribbon upon which the word LIBERTY is inscribed. To the left 7 stars, to the right 6; beneath the bust 1808. The figure 1 is short and above the line of its fellows, the date is much curved and the 08 very close to the border. Front of hair ribbon curved.

Rev.—*Rev. A.*—UNITED STATES OF AMERICA Within a wreath of laurel tied at the stems with a ribbon, ONE | CENT | —— Between ONE and CENT, at a point directly above the upper left corner of the N in CENT is a small dot. The point of the highest leaf terminates below the centre of the final S of STATES. *Measurements*: Distance from the letter D of UNITED to the first S of STATES, and from the final S of STATES to the O in OF, 1⅓; distance from the F in OF to the first A of AMERICA, 1¼. R³. Upon some specimens of this reverse a die-crack appears, beginning at a point on the border above the D of

UNITED, passing through that letter and curving upward through the wreath and the final S of STATES to the border above. Upon still other specimens there is an additional crack beginning at the same point and passing through the left branch of the wreath, irregularly to the letters ON, thence to the right branch of the wreath and terminating at the border between the letters A and M of AMERICA. The die, weakened by these cracks, did its work imperfectly, and the majority of the cents of 1808 are found lightly struck. The lowest star on the left—the one nearest to the bust—is often scarce discernable. Specimens with this imperfection were frequently described by our early cataloguers as the "12 star" variety.

No. 209.

Rev B.

No. 209.—Obv. [Not] Same as No. 208.

Rev.—*Rev. B.*—The point of the highest leaf terminates just below the front line of the final S of STATES. The distance from the D of UNITED to the first S of STATES, from the final S of STATES to the O in OF and from the F in OF to the first A of AMERICA, is 1½ in each instance. R⁴.

The cents of the year 1808 are decidedly scarce even in ordinary condition and fine impressions are rare. The number struck is said to have been 1,109,000.

1809.

The cents of the year 1809 exhibit but one obverse and one reverse. A marked feature is the weakness of the border milling.

No. 210.

Rev. A.

No. 210.—Obv. This obverse is said to have been sunk from the same hub as the die employed in 1808, the 9 at the end of the date having been cut over the 8, in order to hide which it was made larger than the other figures. Traces of the 8 are still visible beneath the 9. A slight defect in the die has left lines extending from the third star on the right to the left, giving the star something of the appearance of a comet with its tail.

Rev.—*Rev.* A.—This is not the same die as *Rev. A* of the cents of 1808, but is now found cracked from the border through the letter T in STATES; the crack passing thence through the tips of the highest pair of leaves to the next leaf on the right. There is also a slight crack above the letter T of CENT. R[5]. ⊗

The 1809 cent is more than scarce in any condition. Usually they are found much worn. Its value in the uncirculated state will be seen when we mention that one of the few perfect specimens known, which was sold with the collection of the Hon. Heman Ely, January 8-10, 1884, realized the high figure of $20.50. The number of cents struck this year is said to have been 222,867. Collectors should be on their guard against clumsy alterations from 1808.

1810

During the year 1810 the type of the two years preceding was maintained. The only marked feature is the employment of the altered die of the preceding year.

⊗ This is not "Rev A" of 1808 as shown by position of leaves in reference to letters of legend. As Rev. A of 1808 was badly broken, Rev. A of 1809 could not be the same unless the 1809 cents were struck first. It differs from all '08's.

No. 211.

No. 211.—Obv. The die is the same as No. 210, the last two figures of the date having been altered to suit the year. The 09 shows very plainly beneath the 10. Length of date through the centre, 5¼. The comet-like tail has been removed from the third star on the right.

Rev.—*Rev. A.*—The point of the highest leaf terminates directly below the front line of the final S of STATES. The distance from the letter D of UNITED to the first S of STATES, from the final S of STATES to the O in OF and from the F in OF to the first A of AMERICA, is 1⅜ in each instance. R^1.

No. 212.—Obv. This is a new die and is usually styled the "Perfect Date." The figures are irregularly placed and widely spaced. Length of date through the centre, 5½.

Rev.—*Rev. A.*—When found in combination with this obverse, *Rev. A* is generally struck too much to the right, which brings the letters ATES of STATES and AM of AMERICA upon the border, making the border on the other side correspondingly broad. R^1.

No. 213.—Obv. Same as No. 212.

Rev.—*Rev. B.*—The point of the highest leaf terminates slightly to the right of the front line of the final S of STATES. *Measurements*: Distance from the letter D of UNITED to the first S of STATES, 1⅜; distance from the final S of STATES to the O in OF, 2; distance from the F in OF to the first A of AMERICA, 1⅜. R^1.

Upon some specimens of this combination the obverse shows a die-crack beginning at the border above the head and passing downward through all the stars on the right, terminating at the 0 in the date. This connected star variety may be classed R[4].

No. 214.—Obv. Length of date through the centre, 5¼. The figures are closer than upon No. 212.

Rev.—*Rev. C.*—The point of the highest leaf terminates more to the right of the front line of the final S of STATES than in any other variety: *Measurements*: Distance from the letter D of UNITED to the first S of STATES, 2; distance from the final S of STATES to the O in OF, 2¼; distance from the F in OF to the first A of AMERICA, 2½. R[3].

The cents of the year 1810 are barely scarce in ordinary condition, and even perfect specimens can be obtained at a moderate price. The number struck is said to have been 1,458,500.

New. C[illegible] close to 214, date 5½, but [illegible]

1811.

The cents of the year 1811 maintain the type originated in 1808. Their peculiar feature is the existence of a variety struck from an altered die of 1810 presenting measurements not found upon any specimen of the issue of 1810 which has come to our notice. It has been suggested that this die was one of the late productions of 1810 and never put into use in its original state. The figures of the date upon this variety are irregularly placed and the final figures 11 found much like the letter I.

No. 215.

No. 215.—Obv. This is the variety struck from the altered die of 1810. The date measures 4½ in length through the centre. The first two figures of the date are on a line, the last two are below this line and inclined at a sharp angle toward the 8. Beneath the final 1 the 0 is distinctly seen.

Rev.—*Rev. A.*—Between the letter E of ONE and the N of CENT a small dash is seen, caused by an imperfection in the die. The highest leaf terminates slightly to the left of the final S of STATES. *Measurements*: Distance from the letter D of UNITED to the first S of STATES, $1\frac{3}{4}$; distance from the final S of STATES to the O in OF, $1\frac{1}{2}$; distance from the F in OF to the first A of AMERICA, $1\frac{3}{4}$. R^4.

No. 216.

No. 216.—Obv. This is the perfect date. The figures are widely but evenly spaced and the 1 in each instance is perfectly formed. The central measurement is 3. The 11 stand slightly below the line of the 18. A slight scratch in the die beginning at the fifth star on the left extends obliquely downward to a point midway between the star and the nose.

Rev.—*Rev. B.*—This is the same die as *Rev. B* of the cents of 1810, to the description of which the collector is referred. R^3.

The cents of 1811 are scarce in any condition and in fine preservation, rare. Collectors are cautioned against clumsy alterations from the cents of 1814. The issue is said to have been 218,025.

1812.

The type of the preceding years was maintained during 1812. The notable distinctions are the large date, of which there are two varieties, the small date and the variety presenting a die-crack which connects all the stars and the figures of the date.

No. 217.—Obv. The figures of the date are large, the 8 particularly so. The second 1 is below the lines of its fellows. The central measurement is 4½, and the distance from the figure 2 to the nearest star, 1¼.

Rev.—*Rev. A.*—The highest leaf terminates ~~below~~ the front line of the final S of STATES. The letters TATES and AMER are usually found touching the border. A line connects the perpendicular strokes of the letter N of CENT. *Measurements*: Distance from the letter D of UNITED to the first S of STATES, 1⅓; distance from the final S of STATES to the O in OF, 1⅞; distance from the F in OF to the first A of AMERICA, 1⅝. R[1].

No. 218.

No. 218.—Obv. The figures of the date are large and well curved. The central measurement is 5 and the distance from the figure 2 to the nearest star, 1½. It is a matter of regret that our illustration of this variety is imperfect. The figure 2 is entirely too large and the length of the date insufficient.

Rev.—*Rev. B.*—The point of the highest leaf terminates below the centre of the space between the final S of STATES and the O in OF. *Measurements*: Distance from the letter D of UNITED to the first S of STATES, 1½; distance from the final S of STATES to the O in OF, 2½; distance from the F in OF to the first A of AMERICA, 2¼. R[1].

No. 219.—Obv. The figures 181 are small and slightly curved. The central measurement is 4¾ and the distance from the figure 2 to the nearest star, 1½. Upon well preserved specimens a slight imperfection in the form of a scratch may be seen on the head.

Rev.—*Rev. C.*—The highest leaf terminates just below the front line of the final s of STATES, ~~as on No. 217~~. The letters TATES and AMER touch the border. *Measurements*: Distance from the letter D of UNITED to the first S of STATES, 1½; distance from the final S of STATES to the O in OF, 1½; distance from the F in OF to the first A of AMERICA, 1⅓. R[1].

No. 220.—Obv. The figures of the date are small, the first 1 stands above the line of its fellows. The central measurement is 4⅜. A die-crack encircling the head connects all the stars and the figures of the date.

Rev.—*Rev. D.*—This reverse is from the same die as *Rev. A* of the cents of 1811, to the description of which the collector is referred. R[3].

The cents of 1812 are quite common and are easily obtained in fine condition. The number issued is said to have been 1,075,500.

1813.

There was no change of type during the year 1813. There are but three varieties presenting only slight differences in the measurements.

No. 221.

No. 221.—Obv. Length of date at top, 5; distance from the top of the figure 3 to the point of the nearest star, 1⅜.

Rev.—*Rev. A.*—The highest leaf in the wreath terminates immediately below the front line of the final S of STATES. *Measurements*: Distance from the letter D of UNITED to the first S of STATES, 1¼; distance from the final S of STATES to the O in OF, $1\frac{1}{2}$; distance from the F in OF to the first A of AMERICA, $1\frac{1}{2}$. R^4.

No. 222.—Obv. Length of date at top, 5, The figures are widely and evenly spaced, the 8 is slightly below the line of its fellows. Distance from the top of the figure 3 to the nearest star, 1.

Rev.—*Rev. B.*—The highest leaf terminates to the right of the final S of STATES. *Measurements*: Distance from the letter D of UNITED to the first S of STATES, $1\frac{1}{2}$; distance from the final S of STATES to the O in OF, $2\frac{1}{4}$; distance from the F in OF to the first A of AMERICA, $2\frac{1}{4}$. Many specimens of this combination are found weakly struck at the upper stars in front of the head and upon the reverse at the word UNITED. R^3.

No. 223.—Obv. Same as No. 221.

Rev.—*Rev. B.*—R^4.

The cents of 1813 are scarce in any condition and in fine preservation rare. The number struck is said to have been 418,000.

1814.

The cents of the year 1814 present no change of type. There are but two varieties, the distinction upon the obverse being in the last figure of the date, which in one instance has a crosslet absent in the other variety.

No. 224.

No. 224.— Obv. *Measurements*: Length of date through the centre, $5\frac{1}{2}$; distance from the top of the figure 4 to the nearest star, $1\frac{1}{3}$. The 4 is small and has a crosslet.

Rev.—*Rev. A.*—The highest leaf terminates to the right of the front line of the final S of STATES. *Measurements*: Distance from the letter D of UNITED to the first S of STATES, $1\frac{3}{8}$; distance from the final S of STATES to the O in OF, $1\frac{3}{4}$; distance from the F in OF to the first A of AMERICA, $1\frac{1}{2}$. R[1]. French Claim. 2 Revs. E:14.- + small Size States.

No. 225.

No. 225.—Obv. *Measurements*: Length of date through the centre, $5\frac{1}{3}$; distance from the top of the figure 4 to the nearest star, $1\frac{1}{8}$. The 4 is large and has no crosslet.

Rev.—*Rev. B.*—The highest leaf terminates immediately below the front line of the final S of STATES. *Measurements*: Distance from the letter D of UNITED to the first S of STATES, $1\frac{1}{3}$; distance from the final S of STATES to the O in OF, $1\frac{1}{4}$; distance from the F in OF to the first A of AMERICA, $1\frac{2}{3}$. R[2]. Upon some specimens of this combination a die-crack appears, beginning at a point on the border below the figure 8, passing through the figure and the hair, thence through the third star on the right to the border beyond. Upon still other specimens a defect under the chin is visible, sometimes slight, at others extending the entire length of the chin to the mouth.

The cents of 1814 are quite common and easily obtained in fine condition. The number struck is said to have been 357,830.

1815.

There were no cents coined during the year 1815.

The year 1814 marks the termination of the fourth series of the cents of the United States. Beyond this date the interest of the majority of collectors does not extend to a degree which makes it desirable to continue the detailed description in which we have hitherto indulged.

Subsequent to 1814 no rare types exist, and but two years, 1823 and 1857, are notable for having produced cents which can be even termed scarce.

For these reasons we shall now discontinue detailed description and present the remainder of the series in the form of tables which we trust may prove at once comprehensive and useful to all collectors of the cents of the United States.

With the year 1857 the issue of the "old red cent" ceased. A movement in this direction was made in 1856 by the issue of the Flying Eagle pattern cent in nickel, to be adopted as the regular coinage in 1857.

During the latter part of 1857, and throughout the year 1858, the Flying Eagle cent held the field, giving place in 1859 to the Indian Head, the present type, with ONE | CENT upon the reverse within a laurel wreath. In 1860 the reverse was changed. Here ONE | CENT appears within an oak wreath which is divided at the top by a small shield and tied below by a ribbon enclosing three arrows and six tobacco leaves.

The use of nickel continued until 1864; the latter part of that year being marked by the appearance of the bronze cent, which has continued in use down to the present time without alteration of type.

Of the small cents, the Flying Eagle of 1856 struck in pure nickel is the rarest, the same in copper slightly less so, and even the specimen in mixed metal which entered into circulation is rare. The 1858 and 1859 cents in copper can only be regarded as patterns, since they never entered into circulation. The issues of subsequent years are entirely common, with the sole exception of 1877, which of late has become scarce.

To the numismatist of the future must be left the comparison of the dies of these later years.

FINIS.

Table No. 1.

Types, Dies, Variations and Combinations, 1816 to 1839.

In general appearance the type adopted in 1816 was maintained until 1839, in which year an entirely different head was introduced As our illustrations present specimens of each year's issue, no detailed description will be attempted. During this period numerous variations appear in the different dies employed each year a few being of sufficient importance to demand classification as separate types. No high degree of rarity is attached to any cent of this period, though certain varieties are much more difficult to obtain than others. The cents of 1823 are the rarest struck during these twenty-four years.

Date.	No. of Types	Name of Types	No. of Obv. Dies.	No. of Rev. Dies.	Variations.	No. of Combinations.	Degree of Rarity.	Remarks.
1816	1	....	5	6	Star distant from 6; Star close to 6; Long date; Close date;	8	R1. R3.	....
1817	2	13 Stars. 15 Stars.	14	11	Divided date; Connected date; Long date; Close date; Star distant from 7; Close stars, two varieties	16	R1. R3.	Four positions of curl: entirely over 1; partly over 1; between 1 and 7 over 7; several badly broken dies.
1818	1			6	Long date; Longest date; Close date; Close stars; Double Chin; Broken Rev.; Close OF.	10	R1. R3.	Several badly broken dies.
1819	2	Over 1818. Perfect Date.		8	Large date; Small date; Long small date; Longest small date; Close small date; Distant stars; Connected stars.	10	R1. R3.	One variety shows double outline on R of AMERICA.
1820	2	Over 1819. Perfect Date.	11	11	Irregular date over 1819; Large date over 1819; Large date; Small date; Long large date; Longest large date; Long Small date; Close date; Long 1; Perfect 2; Twisted 2; Connected stars.	11	R1. R2	The connected star variety is the one usually found bright uncirculated.
1821	1	......	2	2	Long date; Short date; Short date from the broken die.	2	R1. R3.	On the long date variety there is a faint circle seen close to the border extending all around the coin. Long date scarce. Rare fine.
1822	1		10	11	Long date; Short date; Close date; Spread date; Distant star; Cracked obverse; Double UNITED; Close UNITED; Encircled stars.	12	R1. R2.	Scarce fine.
1823	2	Over 1822 Perfect Date.	2	2	3 over 2; Perfect date; Broken border.	2	R2. R4.	Number coined is said to have been 12,250. Rev. of 3 over 2 from die of 1822; rare fine; collectors warned against fraudulent restrike.
1824	2	Over 1822 Perfect Date.	4	4	4 over 2; Long date; Short date; Separated date; Rev. of 1822, distinguished by a crack connecting the bases of all the letters of legend	4	R1. R2.	On " Long Date " are two cracks
1825	1	......	8	8	Long irregular date; Long date with close star; Short date; Short date with close star; Divided date; Double 5; Defective T in CENT.	8	R1. R2.	Several broken dies; widely differing measurements. Scarce fine.
1826	1		[illegible]	6	Leaning 8; Star distant from 1; Double 8; Encircled stars.	10	R1. R3.	Scarce fine.
1827	1		8	5	Open mouth; Star distant from 1; Encircled stars.	11	R1. R2	....
1828	1		3	7	Large date; Small date.	7	R1. R..	....
1829	1		6	7	Large date; Small date; Stars distant from date; Encircled stars	[illegible]	R1. R2.	There are two cracked dies
1830	1		7	[illegible]	Star close to 1; Star distant from 1; Encircled stars.	[illegible]	R1. R2.	Scarce fine
1831	1		6	7	Connected stars; Stars close to date; Slanting date; Large 8.	11	R1. R2.	.. ..
1832	1		[illegible]	3	Open date; Close date; Fallen 8; Large reverse legend; Small reverse legend.	3	R1.	....
1833	1		6	5	High date; Low 8; Cracked reverse; Curl near first 3.	6	R1.	......
1834	1		[illegible]	5	Small 4; Tall 4; Small date; Half and half (18 large 34 small); Connected stars; Cracked reverse.	5	R1.	....
1835	1		7	4	Small date; Half and half (18 large 35 small); Star distant from 1; High curl; New head; Small stars	[illegible]	R1.	The " New Head " presents a facial expression entirely different from the preceding heads of this type.
1836	1		[illegible]	6	Border broken above sixth star; Border broken between seventh and eighth star; Large date; Small date; Straight date; Curved date.	6	R1. R2	Scarce in very fine condition.
1837		Plain hair string Beaded hair string.	11	10	Close date; Large date; Small date; No hair in front of forehead; Double 8; Double 1; No dot between ONE and CENT; One dot; Two dots.	12	R1.	Several cracked dies.
1838	1			4	Cracked Obv.; Double 1; Heavy 1; Crooked 1; Small 8; Large LIBERTY; Curl projecting over forehead; One dot between ONE and CENT; Two dots.		R1.	
1839	5	Over 1836. Head of 1838. Silly Head. Booby Head. Head of 1840.	7	[illegible]	9 over 6; two varieties of Head of 1838; one variety of Silly Head; three varieties of Booby Head, all without dash under CENT; one variety of Head of 1840.	[illegible]	R1. R.	Plate II, No. 1 is Head of 1838, No. 2, Silly Head; No. 3, Booby Head; No. 4, Head of 1840

TABLE NO. 2.

TYPES AND VARIATIONS, 1840 TO 1857.

The last head of Liberty adopted in 1839 continued upon the cents until the latter part of 1843, when a new design made its appearance, presenting a bolder head executed in the same general style, with larger lettering and wreath upon the reverse. This type was continued until 1857, in which year the large copper cent was issued for the last time. During this period of eighteen years the variations of the different dies were too slight to demand even the brief notice bestowed upon the issues of the period preceding. The prominent differences which we note below will afford the ordinary collector sufficient guidance for the arrangement of his cabinet, and at the same time serve as a valuable aid to such as may desire to continue a vigorous distinction of dies to the end of series. The cents of 1840, 1841, 1842, 1843, 1844, 1845, 1846, 1847 and 1848, though common in ordinary preservation, are hard to obtain in the uncirculated state, those of the remaining years of this period can easily be found bright red.

DATE.	No. of TYPES	VARIATIONS.	Degree of RARITY.	REMARKS.
1840	2	Large date. Small date. Large date differences: Curl over 4; Curl to right; Widely spaced date; Close date; 4 touching figures on either side; 4 touching 0 only; 4 touching 8 only; Fallen 8. Small date differences: Curl above 4 (scarce); Curl to right; curl to left.	R1. R2.	8 varieties of the large and 4 of the small date.
1841	1	Differences slight	R1.	5 varieties.
1842	2	Large date; Small date. Differences very slight	R1.	2 varieties of the large and 5 of the small date.
1843	3	1st type. Head and reverse of 1842. 2nd type. Head of 1842, reverse of 1844. 3rd type. Head and reverse of 1844. On 1st type coronet points at fifth star, legend is in small letters. On 2nd type legend and value are in large letters. On 3rd type coronet points between fifth and sixth stars.	R1. R2.	4 varieties of 1st type; 2 varieties of 2nd type; 2 varieties of 3rd type.
1844	1	Differences slight	R1.	6 varieties.
1845	1	Differences slight	R1.	7 varieties.
1846	2	Large date; Small date. The figure 6 is imperfect upon all specimens of the small date.	R1.	12 varieties of the large and 3 of the small date.
1847	1	Differences slight	R1.	14 varieties.
1848	1	Differences slight	R1.	14 varieties.
1849	1	Differences slight	R1.	12 varieties.
1850	1	Differences slight	R1.	10 varieties.
1851	1	Differences slight	R1.	15 varieties.
1852	1	Differences slight	R1.	14 varieties.
1853	2	Over 1852. Perfect date. Other differing points slight	R1. R5.	20 varieties. The altered date is very rare.
1854	1	Star distant from 4; Star close to 4; other differing points slight	R1.	18 varieties.
1855	2	1st type, slanting 55. Differences: Stars perfect; Sixth star faint; Die broken above the ear. 2nd type, Straight 55. Differences slight.	R1. R2.	3 varieties of 1st type, 8 varieties of 2nd type—the latter most easily obtained.
1856	2	1st type. Slanting 5. 2nd type. Straight 5. Differences slight	R1.	5 varieties of 1st type, 5 varieties of 2nd type.
1857	2	Large date; Small date	R3.	2 varieties.

PLATE I.

1816
1817
1817
1817
1817
1817
1817
1817
1818
1818
1819
1820
1820
1821
1822

PLATE II.

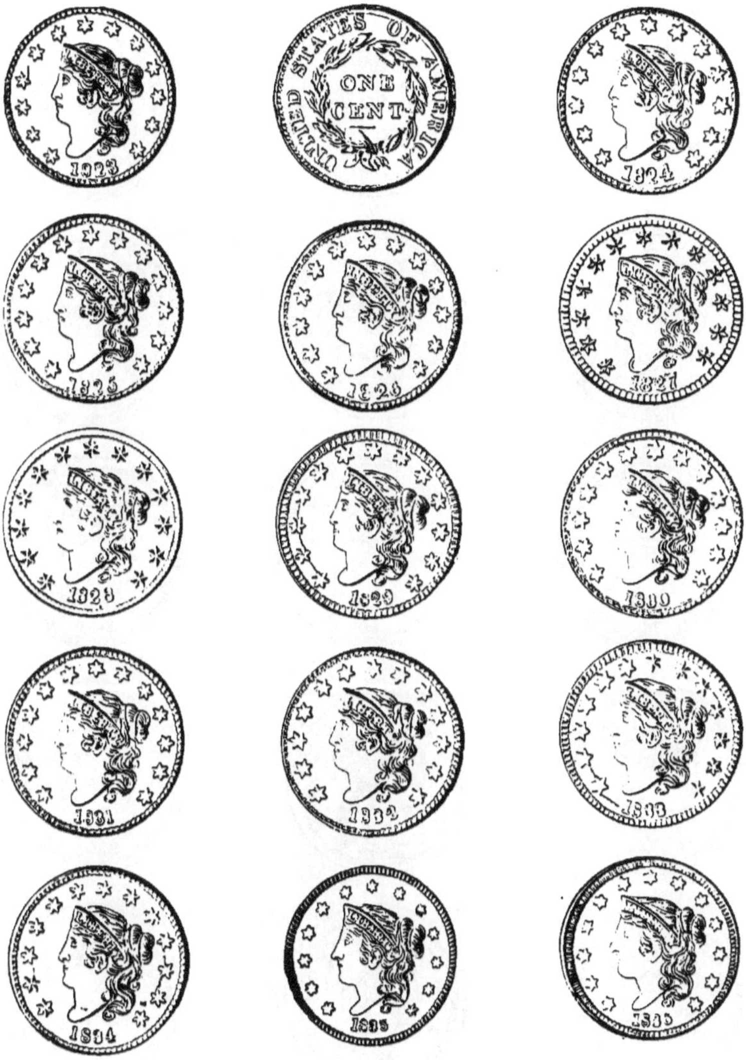

PLATE III.

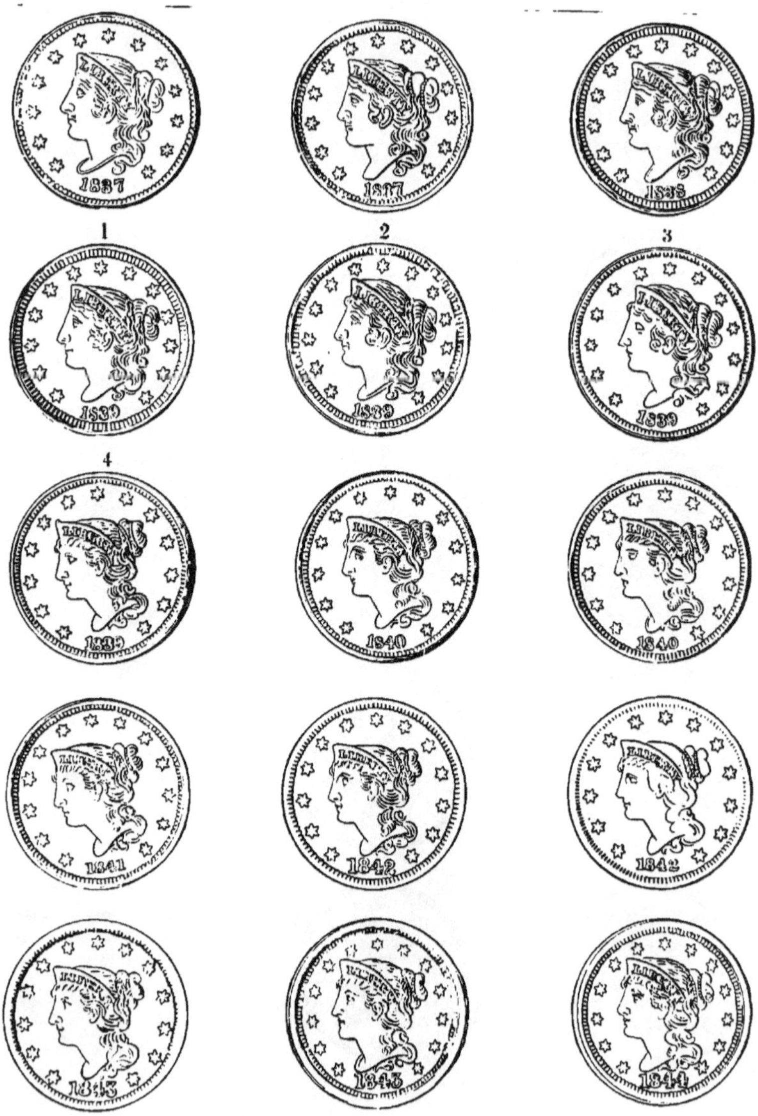
1837
1837
1838
1
2
3
1839
1839
1839
4
1839
1840
1840
1841
1842
1842
1843
1843
1844

PLATE IV.

1845
1846
1847
1848
1849
1850
1851
1852
1853
1854
1855
1855
1856
1857
1857

www.ingramcontent.com/pod-product-compliance
Lightning Source LLC
Chambersburg PA
CBHW020057170426
43199CB00009B/308
* 9 7 8 3 7 4 2 8 6 0 1 7 0 *